3/90
Hoath.

To our parents

Philip Holder

CAPTAIN MAHJONG

OMF BOOKS ◇ LONDON

First published 1976

ISBN 0 85363 113 1

Cover design and illustrations: John Rawding

*Published by the Overseas Missionary Fellowship,
Newington Green, London N16 9QD
and printed in Great Britain by
The Camelot Press Ltd, Southampton*

CONTENTS

AUTHOR'S PREFACE

The Republic of the Philippines is a relatively unknown country to most western people, and those who have visited these beautiful and hospitable islands have not always been privileged to experience life in rural areas far from the roar and bustle of the larger cities.

This book gives a few glimpses of life at the grassroots of the nation. The Filipino people suffered 350 years as a Spanish colony, during which time Roman Catholicism became absorbed into the customs and culture of the people. But in 1898, with the help of the United States, they successfully rebelled, and after the nightmarish Japanese occupation during World War II they became fully independent in 1946.

These stories are Philippine parables, based upon some of the parables of Jesus. They span the period between the Japanese occupation and the declaration of martial law in 1972, when a new epoch of Philippine history began with extensive political, economic and social reforms.

Santo Domingo and Sampaguita are fictional places and all the people and situations depicted in thse stories are imaginary. They are, however, typical of life in a Filipino *barrio* (village) and small country town, and the events related have a strong basis in reality.

Finally I must thank Dr A. J. Broomhall, for ten years OMF Superintendent in the Philippines, for his help and encouragement in the writing of this book.

P. H.

1 CAPTAIN MAHJONG

A burly fisherman peered round the door into the crowded room, where a hissing pressure lamp lit the blue haze of cigarette smoke. "Well done Captain!" he bellowed.

"Ah! Come in, Pedro! Join the celebration!" Dading replied, waving him in with a bottle of beer in one hand and a packet of cigarettes in the other. "Berting," he called to his younger son, "Give Pedro a San Miguel. Pedring, bring up another crate. This one is almost empty."

Dading Aranas, the newly-elected captain of Santo Domingo, a picturesque seaside *barrio* (village), was treating his supporters to the traditional celebration of a successful candidate.

In his coveted position as headman he would be responsible for law and order in the village, he would advise on problems, try to settle quarrels, do what he could to improve the village, and take a leading part in social events.

Dading was an energetic and enterprising man. During the second World War he had fought with the combined American and Filipino forces in the Bataan peninsula against the invading Japanese, and was fortunate to be one of the survivors of the notorious Death March. After the surrender of the Japanese and his consequent release from a prisoner-of-war camp, his poor physical condition, aggravated by frequent bouts of dysentery, had prevented him from joining the Filipino guerrilla forces in the mountains, but he had assisted them whenever possible.

When the liberating American forces arrived and set up a supply depot near Santo Domingo, Dading was able to secure a job in their camp as a barber. After years of hardship under the Japanese, his suddenly increased earnings radically changed his family's economic situation. The generous GI's, ignorant of the value of their money locally, tipped their barber as if they were still in the States. Many of his fellow employees at this time frittered away their large earnings in gambling and wasteful luxuries. Dading, however, saved his money carefully and invested it in land. He was never to regret this foresight and wisdom.

Tessie, Dading's wife, ably supported her husband and resourcefully did what she could to increase the family's income. After the birth of their two boys, Pedro and Alberto (Pedring and Berting to everyone), she opened a *sari-sari* store. As their house was built on stilts, it was relatively easy to wall in part of the space beneath it to make a small shop. With little more than a counter and a few shelves it was surprising how much she earned.

She sold a wonderful array of household needs, a little bit of everything: tinned milk for babies or to add to coffee on special occasions; brown sugar, sold in small quantities wrapped in newspaper cones; coffee and matches; candies, the irresistible temptation for children; candles and starch; bread rolls early in the morning, and hard tasteless biscuits and buns for snacks; bananas, tomatoes and vegetables; "Colgate", whose virtual monopoly made the trade name the Filipino equivalent of "toothpaste"; tiny packets of "Tide" which everyone bought for her laundry; notebooks and pencils for the school children; toilet soap, cigarettes, bottles of soft drinks and beer, and a supply of kerosene to be sold every evening when a stream of children brought bottles for their night's supply; fish-hooks; and vinegar, salt and rice. If you wanted anything you went to the *sari-sari* store and the chances were that Tessie would be able to find it somewhere among her wares.

Always handy was a well-thumbed notebook in which she listed debts, which were numerous and always very difficult to collect. Debts were frequently the cause of bad feeling among some of the villagers who were reluctant to pay. Bad debts at her store were all too common, but Tessie persisted patiently with her shopkeeping.

Dading, with an eye for business, had added to their home a simple lean-to with a table and four short benches. It made an adequate gambling den, and *mahjong* was the favourite game. As operator of the den, Dading took a percentage of the bets, and trade in the shop was encouraged as gamblers bought beer and cigarettes while they played. At night and when work was slack on the land, Dading was frequently busy running his sideline.

Often during the late afternoon several housewives would bring their smaller children to the shop to chat while busily stitching exquisite embroidery. Sometimes they would relax playing bingo or listening to highly-emotional dramas on Tessie's transistor radio. She always played it at full volume as a community service.

One July afternoon in 1958 a game of bingo was in full swing. A group of women and older children, some sitting on a bench, others crouching on the ground, were using pebbles to block out the numbers on their well-worn, soiled cards as the numbers were called, when Lita arrived.

She stood watching with her bare-bottomed children, one on her hip and the other held by its hand. When the game was finished, unable to contain her news any longer, she asked, "Have you heard about the Americanos in Sampaguita?" Sampaguita was their market town, three miles away.

Enquiring eyes were fixed on her, as she had hoped. "No," someone answered for them all. "What's happened?"

"An Americano family has moved into Mr Romulo's

house," she announced. All foreigners are called "Americanos" in the Philippines.

"What are they going to do?" asked a wrinkled grandmother. "Open a factory?"

Immediately visions of well-paid employment for husbands and relations sprang to everyone's mind.

"They are missionaries!" replied Lita, pleased to be the fount of information.

"Catholics?" several asked.

"No, not Catholics. I don't know what they are," answered Lita.

"Well, if they aren't Catholics their teaching must be from the devil. I wouldn't listen to anything not authorized by the Church!" declared Floring, who had been a catechist in her youth, before she married Pedro, the burly fisherman.

That evening Tessie mentioned Lita's news to Dading. "Who are these Americanos in Sampaguita?" she asked.

"I saw one of them in town this morning," he replied. "They speak Filipino very well. They are Protestant missionaries."

"Protestants?" Tessie looked anxiously across at him. "That's bad. It must be. Father Areta says it's a mortal sin to listen to their teaching."

"Oh, Father Areta!" laughed Dading. "You don't have to believe everything he says. Everyone thinks his own religion is the right one, and all the others are wrong. I don't really know what they believe, but when I worked in the army camp I knew some Protestant GIs. They were good fellows. They didn't have the usual vices. They kept out of night clubs and didn't smoke, drink or gamble. They invited me to what they called 'Bible studies'. I went along a few times, but I couldn't understand very much. My English wasn't good enough in those days."

Tessie was curious. "You've never told me that before," she said. "Do they have mass like us?"

"No, I don't think so," he yawned.

"But all our people have been Catholics for hundreds of years, ever since the Spaniards came," she went on. "It would be very bad to change our religion. Don't you think so?"

"I think I'd like some supper," replied Dading, sitting down at the table. "There you are talking about religion, and I haven't eaten yet."

A few weeks later Dading was shirtless, chopping firewood, when the Americanos turned up.

"Good afternoon," Jim Evans called. "Is this the house of Captain Aranas?"

Dading straightened up. "I am Captain Aranas," he replied, with the dignity he had whatever he was doing. Putting his axe down he led the way up the steps. Removing their shoes at the bottom, Jim and Betty followed him up and into the *salas*.

"Sit down," he invited, indicating the varnished mahogany armchairs and settee, and then disappeared to find his shirt.

A group of excited neighbourhood children and a few adults shyly climbed the steps and stood staring in the doorway.

A command from Dading when he returned, and some biscuits and Coca-cola were brought up from the shop below. "Help yourselves," he said, putting them on the low centre table and pushing it closer to them. "I'm sorry, but we haven't any ice here in Santo Domingo. It's a hot day."

In his house down the road, Erning Reyes saw them arrive and could not restrain his curiosity. Self-important, he hurried over to Dading's, pushed his way through the group at the doorway and sat down in the vacant chair. Being a village councillor, he felt that he had a place in any discussion of importance.

"Mr and Mrs Evans," introduced Dading. "This is one of my councillors, Mr Ernesto Reyes."

"Glad to meet you," they said.

"They are missionaries," Dading continued. "They've

recently come to Sampaguita. They are asking if they can give
out leaflets about the Bible in our village. And they want to
teach about God. I told them they're welcome in Santo
Domingo and as far as I'm concerned all teaching about God
is good. It's when people forget about God that the trouble
starts.''

"Are you Protestants?" asked Erning pointedly.

"Yes, we are," answered Jim. "We believe that the Bible is
God's book and that Jesus is the only Saviour, and that if we
believe in Him our sins will be forgiven."

"We all believe in God here," Erning said pompously.

Jim passed them some tracts. "There are the leaflets we
would like to distribute," he said. "I thought you'd like to see
them first. I'm sure you will find them interesting. Where do
you think will be the best place to hold our meeting?"

"You can hold it outside my shop if you like," volunteered
Dading, eager to see what would happen. The neatly-swept
yard edged with a magnificent display of pink, orange, red
and lavender bougainvilia and shaded by a large mango tree
made an ideal meeting place.

"That's very kind of you," said Jim. For ten or fifteen
minutes they chatted together. Then Jim said, "We've
interrupted your work, Captain. If you don't mind we'll go
now and give out these leaflets, and invite people to come
here. We'll be back in about an hour. Is that OK?"

Like Pied Pipers followed by a score of children, Jim and
Betty Evans went from house to house chatting with the
villagers. The tracts were well received, and some said that
they would come to the meeting. But, as expected, a large
group of children and only a few adults turned up.

Dading sat inconspicuously on a sack of rice inside. Tessie,
who had protested volubly to her husband after the
missionaries left, was busy in the kitchen. She was afraid of
committing a mortal sin by hearing Protestant teaching, and
angry with Dading for allowing the meeting to take place
outside their house.

Dading ordered some of the older boys to go up into the house and bring a couple of benches. Before long his memories of his GI friends were being revived, and before they went home to Sampaguita Dading invited Jim and Betty to come again. And so the meeting outside the *sari-sari* store became a regular feature.

One evening Dading apologized for the poor attendance. "You know, in this village we have some fanatical Catholics, mostly school teachers and catechists," he said. "They are telling the children they will go to hell if they attend your meetings. I'm a Catholic myself, but I am tolerant of other religions. I think people should be given a chance to learn about all religions and choose the best."

The following week almost no one came. The weather was dull and cold, and while Betty and Jim waited at the shop front a heavy downpour of rain started.

"Come inside," invited Dading. "You're going to get wet there. And you too," he added to a couple of men who were sheltering with them.

They were shown into the gambling den and sat around the table chatting. After a while Jim said, "It looks as if the meeting's off tonight. I've brought some Bibles. Shall we read a bit?"

Dading liked the idea. And so began a weekly Bible study with a handful of interested people attending fairly regularly. But Pedring and Berting, Dading's teenage boys, could not have cared less, and Tessie continued antagonistic.

"I'm surprised at you, listening to all this Protestant nonsense," she said accusingly to Dading one day. "What would your family say if they were still alive? With a background like yours, you should know better!"

Dading laughed. "Yes, my grandma was very religious. She always said prayers at five o'clock in the morning, and when we stayed with her we had to join in. Her great desire was that I should become a priest."

"And now look at you! You haven't been to mass for years," Tessie added.

"Well," protested Dading, "It's a good thing for you that I didn't take holy orders. We couldn't be married if I were a priest!"

"You men won't take your religion seriously!" she retorted.

"My mother had the same idea," he continued. "Every Sunday when I was a little boy she took me to mass dressed in the robes of St Francis. It's the nearest to being a saint I ever achieved," and he laughed at the memory.

"Oh, you're incorrigible!" Tessie protested. "The trouble with you men is that you only go to church when you are courting, because your girl friends go. You go to Mass and *novinas* and everything then. But once you get married you drop it all. And now you let the Protestants teach their heresies in our home!"

In spite of Tessie and the demands of his nightly *mahjong* club, Dading continued to take an interest in the Bible.

Sometimes when Jim arrived, a game of *mahjong* was in progress, but Dading would stop it and make way for him. Afterwards he would sit and chat with him long after the others had gone, asking for explanations or simply enjoying Jim's company.

One night Jim came home late and could not wait for Betty to brew the usual nightcap. "Stop pottering about!" he said impatiently. "Sit down for a minute. I want to tell you what Dading's been telling me this evening about his brother Leon's experience in the war."

2 NOT A LAUGHING MATTER

The first streaks of dawn were lighting the eastern horizon,
back in October 1944, fourteen years earlier, when Dading's
brother Leon awoke. He stretched and lay still for a few
moments, then throwing off his sheet, he crawled out from
under his mosquito net.

Making his way towards the door he crouched to avoid the
strings of other mosquito nets. The primitive door of palm
leaf shingles tied with rattan to a bamboo frame opened
noisily as it slid along the bamboo pole from which it was
suspended.

Descending the creaking, irregular bamboo steps he
fumbled to find his wooden clogs among the assorted
footwear by the bottom step. Slipping his feet into them he
made his way to the pump.

The air outside felt fresh and cool. A heavy dew lay on the
grass, sprinkling his feet as he shuffled along. A rusty tin full
of water had been left on a stone beside the pump which was
surrounded by a permanent pool of mud. Priming the pump,
Leon rinsed his face, arms and legs. The water felt pleasantly
warmer than the chill morning air. He filled the tin and
replaced it. Drying himself on a towel he made his way back to
the house.

Going into the kitchen, he groped for the matches to light
the fire. "A good cup of coffee will be just the thing," he
thought.

The light of day was increasing rapidly and he could hear the other members of the household beginning to stir. As it was the time of rice harvest, his parents' home was filled to capacity with relations and friends, all eager to earn as much rice as possible, for these were hard times and food was scarce.

Leon himself was frequently away from Santo Domingo. Since the Pacific war had begun to turn in the Allies' favour and American forces had landed on the island of Leyte that same month, the Filipino guerrillas of which he was a member had been much more active. As a courier and intelligence agent he was often away from home for prolonged periods. He was glad to be home now for the harvest, the happiest time of all, when so many relations lived and worked together. They always looked forward to this time with great anticipation.

The smoke from his fire found its way out of the grass-thatched roof and curled upwards to the fronds of the overhanging palm tree. He assembled the thick white china cups, some chipped and cracked, on the bare plank table.

Somehow during the night the ubiquitous ants had found a way across the water moat on a large plate and were swarming into the brown sugar jar. He brushed them off and sweetened the coffee. "We'll get a good early start today," he thought to himself happily.

In the *convento*, the priest's house in the town of Sampaguita, Father Areta was awakened by the insistent ringing of his alarm clock. He slammed down the knob in annoyance. Silence returned. "What an appalling way to start a day! The very devil's invention, alarm clocks," he thought to himself, loath to leave the comfort of his bed.

"Why does mass need to be so ridiculously early? The Protestants certainly have a good idea holding their services at night."

A sense of duty, however, prevailed and reluctantly he

emerged from his mosquito net and sleepily fumbled for his clothes.

Thinking through the programme for his day, he remembered that he was due to conduct mass at Pandayan, a village several miles away on the outskirts of his parish. Afterwards he needed to see the principal of the elementary school concerning the days and hours of his catechists' classes which he hoped to start there soon.

"Oh dear," he grumbled, "another day without a *siesta*."

"Puto! Puto!" The shrill voice of a small boy came closer. Hurrying round the streets, he would soon exhaust his basket of rice cakes, a rare luxury during the Japanese occupation.

Father Areta's mood improved noticeably at the thought of delicious rice cakes liberally sprinkled with freshly-grated coconut.

"I must be quick and buy some of those rice cakes for my breakfast before they are all gone," he muttered to himself. "Now where are my slippers?"

Already the persistent youngster was vigorously knocking on the *convento* door.

"Puto, Father. Rice cakes!"

"I'm coming," he shouted in annoyance. "You don't need to knock the door down."

Not far from the *convento*, in his imposing modern residence, Mayor Abando was enjoying a shower. "The best way to start the day," he thought. "The air is cool but the water feels warm and refreshing."

Due to the poor water pressure in Sampaguita, showers were only possible at night or in the early morning. As soon as the many households started to draw water, the flow dwindled to a trickle and usually stopped altogether. In most homes containers and drums were filled with water at night for the needs of the following day.

In fact Mayor Abando was thinking about this problem

while showering, for today he had an appointment with the Provincial Treasurer and he had hoped some way could be found for releasing provincial funds for his urgent municipal projects.

"I really must improve the water supply," he resolved. So far his administration had accomplished little and his reputation as an effective politician badly needed a boost. "But with everything commandeered by the Japanese for their war effort, what can be done?" he consoled himself.

After an early breakfast he set off in his chauffeur-driven car, appropriate to his dignity, dressed in an expensively embroidered *barong-tagalog* shirt, and accompanied by his municipal treasurer and secretary.

There were exceedingly few vehicles on the road and as he passed by, not a few people wondered, "How does Mayor Abando manage to keep a supply of petrol?" But with a flourishing black market there was no need to investigate too thoroughly.

Mr Tan, a Chinese merchant, opened the front of his shop, the "Sampaguita Trading", and looked across the road towards the high school. In the early morning light he could see the Japanese troops drawn up for inspection on the basket-ball court. Their lorries were standing nearby. They were tough, efficient and hated.

Lt. Watanabe was speaking to his patrol leaders indicating the routes they should follow. The orders were simple—"as usual, root out and destroy all hostile elements".

Their intelligence had informed them that the sizeable guerrilla force that had attacked one of their outposts two nights before was still in the area, and they were determined to exterminate it.

News of the reversals being suffered by their own forces in the Central Philippines made them even more ruthless and vicious than ever before in conducting reprisals. Another sweaty day of trudging through rice paddies and jungle after an elusive foe was a gloomy prospect for them.

"They are still going after the guerrillas!" Mr Tan said to his son. "But I am sure that they are far away by now. The guerrillas only strike when they want to and then they disappear."

"I hope the Japs won't stay in the school much longer," replied his son. "We are missing the trade the schoolboys bring us."

"Go and listen to the Voice of America broadcast. Find out how far the allies have reached," his father instructed, for Mr Tan didn't understand English himself.

His son disappeared into the back of the house to uncover their secretly-hidden radio and then quietly listened to the short wave news bulletin from America.

Mr Tan busied himself tidying up his grocery store and preparing for the day.

Soon the Japanese troops climbed into their trucks and he watched them pull out of the school gates and drive noisily towards the hills.

Not long afterwards he caught sight of Mayor Abando driving by in all his splendour. "Where is the Mayor going today?" he wondered. "It must be an important occasion. He is very smartly dressed."

Business was slow because many of the townspeople were in the country harvesting rice. Mr Tan was relaxing in the breezy doorway of his shop when a horse-drawn *kalesa* trotted by.

"Ah! Father Areta," he said to himself and nodded to the priest. "He must be off somewhere to say mass. It isn't often that he goes out of town. He prefers people to come to him. There must be an important function somewhere."

He turned to his son behind the counter. "I'm going out at noon to visit some contacts," he remarked. "I want to buy as much rice as possible at harvest time while it's still available."

The harvest was going well. The yield was good, and the harvesters, keeping the sun off their skin with wide-brimmed hats and sweat towels, long-sleeved shirts, blouses and jeans, were enjoying themselves. But it was hard work too, cutting off the ears of rice by hand and then trampling out the grain with bare feet.

Leon and his brother Dading had spent several hours threshing the rice with their feet on large woven palm-leaf mats like king-size sleeping mats.

Their mother, still remarkably strong and agile, winnowed the rice, pouring it slowly from a large, round, flat basket. The breeze blew the husks away, leaving the grain to fall on to another woven mat. Whenever the wind stopped she would whistle on a low melancholy note to call it again—and of course was not surprised when it returned!

"It's time we carried some of this rice down to the road," Dading said to Leon, observing the position of the sun. "Take a sack and leave it at Uncle Mauro's house across the bridge. We can pick it up there later with a *kalesa* and take it to Santo Domingo."

Leon agreed and picking up a sack, also woven of palm leaf like the mats, swung it on to his head and started off for the road a considerable distance away.

Reaching the road he turned, crossed the wooden bridge over the river and was jogging towards his uncle's house when he suddenly caught sight of an approaching Japanese patrol.

As he was involved in guerrilla activities, a multitude of questions raced through his mind. "Why are they here? Has someone betrayed me? Are they coming to arrest me?" Thinking like the Irishman that he would rather be a coward for five minutes than a corpse for the rest of his life, he decided to go back over the bridge before they noticed him, and hide until the patrol had passed.

Dropping the sack of rice he ran for the bridge.

Unfortunately the Japanese had seen him. A multitude of questions also raced through Lt. Watanabe's mind. "Who is that man? Why is he trying to evade us? He must be a guerrilla!" he concluded.

His men were already poised. "Fire," he commanded. Shots rang out. Leon fell at the foot of the bridge.

They searched his body but found no incriminating papers.

Only an attractive watch and a little money. Soon they continued their way in single file along the side of the road.

They hadn't gone more than a mile when a car passed them.

"It looks like the Sampaguita contingent," noted Mayor Abando. "They are scouring the area very thoroughly."

"How much longer are they going to be with us?" wondered the treasurer.

"Ah, there is Lt. Watanabe!" exclaimed the mayor, raising his hand to him as they went by. "I wonder what he has been up to today?"

Crossing the bridge the chauffeur braked suddenly. "Look!" he exclaimed excitedly. "There's a man on the verge!"

The passengers involuntarily strained forward.

"Must have just been killed, poor brute! Another victim of our friend Watanabe, I suppose," suggested the municipal secretary.

"Who is he?" asked the mayor, craning his neck to get a better look.

No one recognized him.

"It looks as though he has been harvesting," observed the treasurer. "Goodness knows what he did to deserve death."

"He'll soon be found by his friends," said Mayor Abando, leaning back in his seat. "There is no point in us stopping. Keep going, driver. I don't want to be late for supper."

Father Areta felt drowsy. If it hadn't been for the jolting of the *kalesa* he would probably have gone to sleep. As it was, he held on grimly to the roof support with one hand while the *kalesa* rattled from pothole to pothole.

"What a terrible state these roads are in now," he complained to the driver.

"Nothing has been done to them for a long time," he replied. "The grader broke down a couple of years ago and has never been repaired."

Father Areta shaded his eyes as he looked across the paddy

fields to where a group of harvesters were still hard at work.

A group of children coming out of school politely nodded their heads and called "Good afternoon, Father!" as he passed. He smiled benignly at them.

Eventually they reached a wooden bridge. The horse slowed to a walk on the inclined approach. They crossed slowly to ensure that the *kalesa* wheels kept on the planks laid across the joists.

Suddenly the *kalesa* driver exclaimed, "*Naku*, Father! There's a man there!"

Father Areta looked in astonishment.

"Stop!" he commanded and jumped to the ground.

Together they stared in horror at Leon. "He's been shot," said Father Areta in a loud whisper.

"Must be the Japs," declared the driver.

"Probably," the priest replied. "Look at the blood, poor man, and the ants are on him already."

"What shall we do?" asked the driver looking up and down the deserted road.

"Well, he looks dead," sighed the priest. "There's nothing we can do. If he were alive I could give him the last unction. It's a pity we weren't here earlier."

After saying a prayer for the peaceful repose of his soul, Father Areta climbed back into the *kalesa*.

"Come on!" he called to the driver who was still standing staring at the body. "We have no time to lose. I have a *novina* tonight."

Mr Tan's heavily-loaded *kalesa* was creaking home. Its axles threatened to give up the unequal struggle, the two wheels wobbling drunkenly. He was well satisfied with his business contacts which promised to bring to his mill more rice than he had dared hope for in these days of acute food shortage. He wasn't coming home empty-handed either!

He was a man of few words. Probably because his command of the Filipino language was poor, he rarely spoke to his driver.

Reaching the incline before the wooden bridge the driver jumped down to lighten the load and to hold the horse's bridle while they cautiously crossed on the planks.

He had been watching the wheels to make sure that they stayed on the planks and was surprised when suddenly Mr Tan shouted. "There's a man!"

He turned and saw Leon. They stopped. Mr Tan joined him.

"Is he dead?" asked Mr Tan kneeling over Leon while his driver looked on. Much to his surprise he found that he still had a pulse. "He's still alive!" he declared in amazement.

"Shot by the Japs," ventured the driver.

Mr Tan made no reply. Instead he took off his shirt, tore it into strips and applied what first aid he knew.

"Now let's get him into the *kalesa*," he said, standing and stretching himself.

"But it is loaded with rice!" declared the driver hopelessly.

"Well, unload it then!" ordered Mr Tan.

"What? Here on the road?" queried the slow-thinking driver.

"Yes, of course! We must be quick or this man will die."

"But it will be stolen," argued the driver.

"When a man may die, what is a bit of rice?" shouted the Chinese. "Get it out!"

Obediently the driver unloaded the rice and together, with great difficulty, they hoisted Leon carefully up into the *kalesa*. As they laid him on the slatted floor, Leon groaned and for a moment opened his eyes before falling unconscious again.

"Now, quickly!" commanded Mr Tan. "We must get him into the Santa Maria Clinic immediately.

The jogging was terrible. Mr Tan did the best he could with an empty rice sack to make a pillow for Leon's head.

At last they arrived at the clinic and were met by Dr Maramot.

"Who is he?" asked the doctor. Mr Tan didn't know.

"Who will be responsible for him?" enquired the doctor. Again Mr Tan didn't know.

"You can't bring a patient here and not have someone responsible for him," pointed out the doctor. "Who will authorize the treatment? Who will pay the bills? He may be a guerrilla! What will happen to me if the Japs discover I'm treating a wounded guerrilla?"

"But you must treat him immediately or he will die," insisted Mr Tan. "I'm not going to treat a man who can't pay!" declared the doctor adamantly. "Why don't you call his relations?"

"But we don't know who he is, so how can we know who his relations are?" parried Mr Tan.

"Then go to where you found him and enquire," suggested Dr Maramot.

"But he will die if we delay. His wounds need attending to immediately," asserted Mr Tan. "Might he not need an operation?"

"No guaranteed payment; no treatment! That is our rule here," affirmed the doctor. "And anyway, I have to think of my own security."

Mr Tan was exasperated. Pulling out fifty pesos left from his rice-buying expedition, he handed them to Dr Maramot.

"Here, take this!" he said, pushing the money into his hand. "This is the first payment. Give him the best treatment you can. I'll pay his bills. I'll be back tomorrow to see how he is getting on."

"Well, that was the story Dading told me," Jim said to Betty. She was sitting with her chin in her hands listening round-eyed. She could imagine it all so clearly. Just fourteen years ago. Dading's boys were little more than babies then, she thought. The boys were now full of fun, very like their father.

A few days later Jim and Betty were in Santo Domingo again, sitting in Dading's lean-to. To the great amusement of some friends Pedring and Berting were mimicking the Chinese. "You likey flied lice? Velly nice lice today," Pedring was saying, and Berting joined in: "Old Mr Tan sits in his vest and baggy white trousers at the doorway of the 'Sampaguita Trading'. This is how he talks . . ."

"That's enough!" Dading interrupted. "Talk about Chinese if you like, but I won't have you mock Mr Tan."

The boys fell quiet and listened as Dading went on reproachfully, "Don't you know that if it were not for Mr Tan your Uncle Leon would be dead? Have you forgotten what I told you? How Mr Tan saved his life and paid his hospital bills after he had been shot by the Japanese? That Chinese is a better Filipino than many a Filipino! Who was the true Filipino that day? Was it Mayor Abando who rode past him in his car, or Father Areta who would only say a prayer for his soul, or Mr Tan who took him to hospital and cared for him?" Dading went on rubbing it in as if he was afraid they might forget again one day and hurt Mr Tan's feelings.

"This country would be a much better place if everyone were like Mr Tan. No! I won't hear a word spoken against him."

Dading turned to Jim and Betty and went on, "The shooting of Leon was only one incident among many that made the years of the Japanese occupation of this area a nightmare for all of us. I never pass Juanita's *tuba* stall without remembering all she has gone through. I'll tell you what happened. It was about the same time, when the Americans had landed in Leyte and the Japanese knew they were losing the war. They were dangerous. They would stop at nothing. . . ."

3 THE PERSISTENT PHANTOM

It was June 1944 and Santo Domingo was sweltering beneath angry skies. Dading mopped his face and neck with the ragged hand towel draped over his shoulders like a miniature scarf. Although it was still early in the day, the breathless heat penetrated the dusty open space between the long stilts of the house.

He looked across at Lito, a carpenter when conditions were wrong for fishing, sharpening his plane on a well-worn stone. "The sharper the blade the less you sweat," he commented, removing the towel again and rubbing his arms. "This mahogany sure is hard."

Lito tested the blade with his thumb and, approving, dried it on his trousers before replacing it in his home-made plane.

"It's a pity the other men have gone into hiding," replied Lito. "We could do with a bit of help on this coffin."

Dading adjusted the position of his plank on the bench that had been brought down from the house above them, then, sitting astride again to hold it firm, continued planing.

The two of them worked on in silence, the curled-up dark red shavings falling around their bare feet. Above them they could hear distinctly through the split bamboo floor the hushed voices of the women and the frequent sobs of Juanita. They could hear, too, Floring, the catechist, leading the prayers for Carding's soul.

Squatting on the floor, the women, dressed in black, were keeping vigil around the corpse. It lay on a hand-woven palm-leaf sleeping mat with a smoking oil lamp made out of a beer bottle at its head and, surprisingly, was completely covered with a white sheet. Loving hands wafted away the flies that occasionally alighted on the sheet. Money in the glass jar beside the corpse showed the practical help and sympathy of the mourning friends.

Jun, Juanita's fourteen-month-old son, wearing only a vest, crawled around on the floor, providing a little distraction for the sorrowing group.

Frequently he had to be pulled away when he tried to grab the flickering flame of the lamp or when he ventured too near the corpse of his father. (His name was the same as his father's, so being Ricardo Junior he was known by the abbreviation Jun. Almost everyone is known by an abbreviation of his name.)

In the ample shade of a breadfruit tree, Dading's wife Tessie superintended the cooking of the rice and a couple of chickens. It would be a very simple meal for so many visitors, little more than rice, but food was scarce and she was doing the best she could for her cousin.

Eventually, the planing completed, the sound of sawing and hammering announced the progress of the work under the house. Before noon the simple coffin with its dark brown wood-stain still slightly wet was brought up the steps into the one-roomed house.

The women made way for the men. Without a word being spoken they placed the coffin by the sleeping mat and removed the sheet. Most of the women immediately averted their gaze and wiped their tears. Many wept aloud.

Lito took Carding's feet and Dading his shoulders as they lifted his decapitated corpse into the coffin. Juanita, shrieking, collapsed on the floor as Dading picked up her husband's head and reverently placed it with the body. With Lito's help he secured the lid.

The children who had been playing outside quickly raced up the steps and stood with large round eyes in the doorway observing the scene.

Carding was a victim of Japanese retribution. The previous day a group of Filipino guerrillas had ambushed one of their army lorries as it crossed the river bridge near Santo Domingo. Two soldiers had been killed.

The infuriated Japanese reacted ruthlessly as usual. A patrol immediately searched the area. In their anger every Filipino man was regarded as a guerrilla or guerrilla sympathizer.

Carding was returning from work in his paddy fields. Knowing nothing of the ambush he walked on unsuspectingly towards the approaching Japanese troops.

He was stopped and brutally interrogated. While he, in distraught terror pleaded his innocence, Lt. Watanabe denounced him as a liar, drew his sword and beheaded him beside the track.

A child carrying firewood had found his body. Dropping his load, he had run home in horror with the news.

Leaving the coffin in the centre of the sleeping mat, Dading and Lito withdrew to a corner of the room.

Through a window propped open with a short bamboo pole, Dading caught sight of Juanita's neighbour, Celso, and his helpers arriving from the cemetery. He went out to meet them. "How is it, Celso?" he asked. "Did you have enough cement?"

Celso shook the ash from his crooked, home-made cigarette. "Yes, it's all ready, but we need a bit more board for the roof. I'll take a piece you didn't use," he replied, looking at the untidy jumble of timber under the house.

After lunch another neighbour, Juan, arrived with his *kalesa*. The coffin was loaded into it and Juanita and Carding's mother climbed up to ride with the coffin.

Other women of the family crowded into Celso's *kalesa*, while the rest, with black umbrellas to protect them from the sun, walked with the men.

Slowly the procession made its way to Sampaguita for the last rites at the old Spanish church before proceeding to the cemetery. There, at last, with the tearful prayers of his family, Carding's coffin was pushed into the box-like tomb, built above ground and just big enough to contain it. Quickly cement was mixed, more bricks laid and the tomb sealed.

While the cement was still wet, Dading wrote in it with a twig the inscription, "Ricardo Garcia. June 21, 1944". Underneath he drew a reclining cross with the letters "S.L.N." meaning "*Suma Langit Nawa*", to express the prayer, "May he be in Heaven".

For weeks Juanita was almost inconsolable. Great hatred towards the Japanese grew in her heart. She gave whatever help she could to the guerrillas and longed for the liberation of her homeland. For three years she had recalled General MacArthur's parting words to the Filipino people before he escaped to Australia after the fall of Bataan, "I shall return!" Now, "He has kept his promise," she would say to herself. "The Americans have returned and the Japanese will pay for their atrocities. We shall be free again."

Little did she realize what the liberation would mean for her.

She was weeding in the rice paddies and chanced to look up. She paused in shocked disbelief. Smoke was rising from Santo Domingo.

"*Sunog!* Fire! Fire!" she screamed to her companions. Grabbing little Jun she ran as fast as she could towards the village, fear lending speed to her feet.

But she was too late. When she arrived most of the houses in Santo Domingo had already collapsed in flaming ruins, including her own. In agony she stared at the glowing embers of the house she had left that morning. The heavier timbers were still burning, but of the rest, the bamboo, the palm-leaf roof and walls, and all their possessions, only ashes remained. Everything was burnt.

Old Grandfather Vicente, a neighbour, came over and stood beside her. His house, too, had been destroyed. "The *Japs* did it," he said in a choking voice almost overcome with emotion. "They have gone now. They took your pig and mine too. The Americans will soon be here." He paused, and then added, "It is good that you were not here. At least you and Jun are still alive."

"Our house is burnt," sobbed Juanita. "Oh, Jun, our house is burnt." She squatted down and put her arms around him, her tears falling on his tangled black hair while he stared with uncomprehending round eyes at the destruction and confusion.

Ten years passed and Jun was a robust boy of twelve, happy to spend his time with his friends Pedring and Berting over at Dading's house. But life remained a continual struggle for Juanita. She worked hard on their few acres of land, hiring help for the work she was not able to do herself. And later, to try and earn a little more money, she moved her frail, one-roomed shack to Sampaguita. Led by Dading, always a friend in need, all the men of Santo Domingo rallied to help her. Encouraged with plenty of coconut beer and cigarettes, they tied bamboo poles to the stilts of her palm-leaf and bamboo home and carried it on their shoulders across a field to the road. There they loaded it on to a "six by six"—a strong, flat-backed ex-American army truck—which transported the flimsy house to a little plot of land she had rented near the town *plaza*.

Through the years Juan too had been a good neighbour to Juanita. Now he half carried, half dragged several long bamboos on his *kalesa* into Sampaguita for her, and Lito made them into a bench and what professed to be a counter.

Every afternoon, Juan brought several gallons of *tuba*, a kind of coconut beer, from the plantation and Juanita poured it into large glass containers and took up her position at the counter. The grey-brown frothy drink could be seen to be still fermenting, bubbling and rapidly becoming more potent.

Most of the palm trees in the immediate vicinity were tapped for *tuba*, for the men of Sampaguita town had a great thirst which had to be quenched every evening with gallons of liquor. So Juanita had plenty of customers.

Tuba gatherers are muscular men. Climbing thirty or forty palm trees twice a day, every day, in all weathers, is no job for weaklings. Early in the morning and again in the afternoon, they could be seen doing their rounds. Bare-footed and dressed in no more than shorts and vest, they climbed the high palms one after the other.

As the palm trees grew, the men cut widely spaced notches into the trunks, and climbed quickly to the top with giant steps, expertly swinging themselves up among the fronds. The boys loved to watch them away up there, sitting on the enormous leaves as they did their work. With a razor-sharp, crescent-shaped knife they sliced a thin sliver from the fruit-bearing stem so that the sap dripped continuously into bamboo tubes, three on each palm.

Then down the notched trunk each *tuba* gatherer would climb with a full tube hung over his shoulder by a wooden hook. At the foot of the tree he poured the *tuba* into old kerosene cans and then with the cans dangling from a pole across his shoulder he trotted off to the next palm tree, or to the roadside for Juan or Celso to take in their *kalesas* to the *tuba* stall.

Selling *tuba* was never a pleasant occupation for Juanita. Often the men would stay for hours chatting and arguing together and becoming increasingly drunk. Yet it provided a little additional income to supplement the earnings from her rice paddies, and Jun could attend the better school in the town. When they were available she also sold cooked dog meat and eels, which the men enjoyed as a delicacy to go with their drink.

So time passed, bringing with it few changes to the town of Sampaguita or the village of Santo Domingo. Father Areta continued as priest; Dr Lopez, the bank manager, built himself a magnificent house; Frederico Sarmiento was appointed municipal judge; babies were born and people died and were buried, but for most people life just plodded on.

All judges were appointed by the President of the Philippines and Judge Sarmiento was a political appointee. He was an individualist and seemed not to care what anyone thought of him. He scorned Father Areta and the church and was totally irreligious. Moreover, he was addicted to *mahjong* and almost every evening of the week could be seen seated at a table in his house with Dr Lopez and a few friends, gambling.

On hot airless nights the windows of his house would be wide open and the clatter of the *mahjong* tiles could be clearly heard down the street until the early hours of the morning and not infrequently right through the night. Judge Sarmiento made few friends outside the small élite circle.

In court his high-handed manipulation of the law and arbitrary decisions made him fearsomely unpredictable. He preferred the out-of-court settlement of cases, especially when he was suitably "thanked". It helped to maintain his skill at *mahjong*.

After the war, and until martial law was declared in 1972, the Philippines was not without its opportunists who sought every possible way to exploit their fellow men in order to amass wealth. Litigation over the possession of land and boundaries had always been in vogue, but in those days trouble erupted for poor families as never before. These unscrupulous rogues knew the intricacies of the law, and also the effectiveness of a well-placed bribe.

In this way disaster again overtook Juanita. During the war, records of every description had been destroyed, both those of individual citizens and those in central offices.

Juanita could not believe her ears when one day she was

informed by an employee of Attorney Teodoro Marquez, a wealthy lawyer who owned the land adjoining hers, that she had no right to use the paddy fields she had farmed for so long near Santo Domingo. Legal possession was his.

Juanita was desperate. Without stopping to change out of her soiled "Mother Hubbard" dress, she hurried into the street and caught the next jeepney going to Santo Domingo. Since she had moved to Sampaguita, Dading had been supervising the farming of her land. And now he was the new *barrio* captain of Santo Domingo. Juanita hardly noticed the boys fishing for mudfish in the irrigation channel in front of Dading's house. One of them, with a piece of string tied to a stick, had hooked a bent pin to the skin in the middle of a frog's back and was encouraging it to swim as bait under the foot-bridge, a favourite place for the mudfish to hide.

Juanita hurried across the bridge towards the house. "*Tao po*," she called at the foot of the steps. "There is someone here."

"Come on up, Juanita," replied Tessie, recognizing her cousin's voice. Juanita slipped off her thong sandals and climbed the steep steps.

Tessie and Dading were sitting at the table eating boiled sweet-potatoes and drinking coffee for their afternoon *merienda*.

"Come and join us," invited Dading. "You've chosen the right moment!"

Juanita was so distressed that she was not at all hungry, but she broke off a piece of sweet-potato and nibbled at it, with brown sugar and grated coconut.

They could see how upset she was, so after a few sentences about nothing in particular Dading asked, "How can we help you, Juanita?"

"Oh, Dading, I have a big problem and so I have come to you. You are like a father to me. I need your advice," she replied.

"Well, I'll do what I can," promised Dading.

"You remember our first home here in Santo Domingo which was destroyed by the Japanese," she began.

"Yes, of course," replied Dading, puzzled. "We all lost our homes then. But that was years ago."

"When our home was burned we lost everything," she continued, the tears coming to her eyes. "All my official papers were burnt; the title to our land was among them. During the war all the records at Sampaguita were destroyed too."

"I am beginning to see your problem," Dading said, his lips tightening and his big eyes staring incredulously. "Someone is interfering with the boundary of your land."

"It's worse than that," replied Juanita. "Attorney Marquez, whose land adjoins mine, has obtained new deeds for his own and included my few acres with his!"

"But he can't get away with that!" protested Dading.

"No," replied Juanita, fighting hard to keep the tears back, "but he has a title deed for all my land and I have nothing to prove that I am the true owner."

"We must go and get legal advice", decided Dading. He took a drink of water and stood up. "Where's my new shirt, Tessie?" Then turning to Juanita, he added, "If you like I will go with you; we will see what we can do about it."

The results of their enquiries were disheartening. The first disquieting fact they learned was that Attorney Marquez had already played the same trick on other smallholders. In fact he was reported to have accomplices who were searching out more victims for his cunning.

Once Attorney Marquez had been able to obtain the deeds to the land, he was in a very strong position. Legal procedures were so expensive that a dispossessed farmer was usually compelled to give up the struggle against men like the wealthy Marquez. Without his land the farmer had no source of income for paying a lawyer. Taking the matter to court would accumulate debts and if the poor man lost his case, as he probably would against such an opponent, he would be bankrupt for life.

Dading did the best he could to help Juanita. Returning from yet another unsuccessful visit to a lawyer he slumped into a chair and said to his wife, "Tessie, we have the most despicable set of lawyers in Sampaguita that you could ever imagine. To see them at mass on Sunday mornings you would think that Saint Peter himself would feel honoured to be their shoe-shine boy, but they won't help a poor widow against that land-grabber Marquez."

"I'm sorry," said Tessie with a sigh. "I do wish we could do something to help Juanita. And I hope our own title deeds come through soon, before the same happens to us. It's months since we lodged the application at the Bureau and still we've heard nothing."

"The lawyers all say they would like to help," continued Dading, "but they have wonderful excuses. 'Too busy' they say. They know there's no money in the case. Juanita can't pay big fees. Truth is, they're scared to stand up against Marquez. It's no wonder that some of these farmers take the law into their own hands. I saw in the *Manila Times* yesterday that one of these wealthy land-grabbers was ambushed and killed."

Seeing the hopelessness of her situation, and driven by despair, Juanita did the only thing she could think of. She went to see Judge Sarmiento.

It was a dark night and the street lighting was poor when she hurried along the muddy pot-holed road in her wooden clogs towards the judge's home.

While still several houses away she could hear the noisy clatter of the *mahjong* tiles being shuffled on the table. She immediately realized that this was a most inauspicious time to visit him, while he was engrossed in a game, but she was desperate and proceeded to the house.

Knocking at the open door she called out fearfully, "*Tao po!*"

One of the judge's daughters appeared and invited her in. Then she called her father. A few minutes later he came.

"What is it?" he demanded brusquely, obviously annoyed at being disturbed.

Juanita told him her problem. Time and again she had rehearsed what she needed to say.

"But why come to me? Get a lawyer. That's what they are for!" he snapped and rejoined the game.

Juanita was not to be easily deterred. The next night she was back again.

"No lawyers will handle my case," she informed him.

"Why not?" asked the judge in exasperation.

"Because they don't want to risk opposing Attorney Marquez. And anyway, I haven't any money to pay for a lawyer," replied Juanita. "I'm just a poor widow. Even if I were to win my case I would probably have to sell all my land to pay the fees."

"Well, why do you come back to me?" he asked.

"I want you to help me," she pleaded.

"But how?" demanded the judge.

"By getting my land back for me," she begged.

Judge Sarmiento would take no more from such a stupid woman. Turning to go back to the *mahjong* room, he barked emphatically, "I'm not a prosecution lawyer; I'm a judge! If the lawyers of Sampaguita won't handle your case, then find one somewhere else who will."

But he could not get rid of Juanita as easily as he expected. She reappeared with persistent regularity, for she was convinced that the judge was the only person in the world who could help her. In spite of all the rebuffs and abuse she received from him, she still returned.

"Go away! I don't want to see you again. . . .!"

"Don't let that woman in again! If she comes again, send her away. . . .!"

After several weeks of this, Judge Sarmiento felt that this distraught woman was haunting him. In spite of all the abuse he hurled at her, Juanita refused to lose hope. His reactions had varied from annoyance to amusement, and then to boiling anger, but still on every possible occasion she reappeared to plead her cause and beg his help.

He had never experienced anything like this before. Some people had appealed to him but he had been able to throw them off easily. This widow was different.

As time went on it became even worse—the silent figure like a phantom standing outside his office door; the poor woman with a ragged shawl outside his house, even in her silence most eloquently pleading her cause. And everyone knew it. She was drawing unwelcome attention to him and his own activities.

In the end he decided to act, if only to retain his sanity. He yielded. "All right," he snapped. "Come into my office. I'll help you. Now give me the details of your land. . . ."

He was surprised at the sense of relief he experienced as he took down the information. "I don't care how the politicians react," he thought to himself. "I'm going to see that this widow gets justice!" Self-righteousness could be quite heart-warming.

By then Jim Evans had been visiting peaceful Santo Domingo almost every week for nine months. Dading's welcome was always warm and Tessie had long since lost her prejudice against "those *Protestantes*". The lean-to alongside the *sari-sari* store was still used for gambling, but Captain Mahjong, as the *barrio* often called him, seemed to be losing interest in his cronies' games.

In Sampaguita town several people had already taken to meeting on Sundays to worship together. "After all, this is the real thing," they said to their critics. Father Areta was alarmed. He made a point of warning his congregations against the dangers of listening to heresy. The blindly faithful took heed and kept their distance with appropriate dark looks when they passed the Evans' house. But friendliness speaks

more loudly than words and neither Jim nor Betty were dumb
when opportunities came their way. They helped their
neighbours move house, patiently explained the Gospel to
them, or even stood up and preached at the street corner to
those townsmen who were too curious to be ruled by Father
Areta's warnings. In several *barrios* they began to see curiosity
turning into a desire to understand the Bible. Like Captain
Mahjong himself.

"Why, this isn't a *bad* book!" Dading declared to some men
on the beach one day. "I've been comparing it with the one in
the municipal office that has Cardinal Rufino Santos'
authorization at the front. They are as good as identical.
What's Father Areta talking about?"

So several more of his friends were coming to Jim's study
sessions and asking questions. Lito was one. Even Ernesto
Reyes sometimes joined them.

"You know," Jim said to Betty one evening when he came
home from visiting Captain Mahjong, "I think the time has
come to invite Ramon Ilaw for a few days, to hold special
meetings in Sampaguita and the *barrios*."

They talked it over with the handful of Christians who met
in their home the next Sunday. The idea caught on at once. A
Filipino pastor from Manila would be able to explain things
much more clearly. Jim and Betty did their best, but after all,
they were using an unfamiliar language and could hardly be
expected to understand all the background to the problems
Filipino people faced when they put their faith in Christ.

"I want to ask him whether I can be baptized without
telling my parents," said one, "because they will get mad if I
even hint that I would like to be baptized."

"The thing that bothers me," added another, "is what to
do about Tony. We're engaged but he isn't a believer yet. I'd
like to know what the pastor has to say about that."

So Pastor Ilaw came. And had to prolong his stay.

"Don't go. You've only just come. We want to hear more."

It was the same in Santo Domingo as in Sampaguita town,

and other places too. He spoke so simply and interestingly, with such sparkle and such penetrating illustrations from their daily life. Dading was insatiable.

"Come upstairs," he pleaded when everyone except Ramon Ilaw and Jim had gone home one night. Holding his pressure lamp high to light the steep steps for his guests, he led the way up to his living room. His sons Pedring and Berting had listened for an hour or so earlier in the evening, but for boys in their teens it was all a bit too serious and now they were breathing deeply under a mosquito net in the corner. Tessie was rubbing her eyes when she looked out of the inner room. The old Mother Hubbard she was wearing showed that she was ready for bed too.

Dading led his guests to the table and put out some biscuits and bananas for them. He turned the light down to soften its hissing and glare.

"Tell me," he said quietly lest he wake the boys. "Did I understand when you were talking about Jesus and that lawyer man, Nicodemus? Isn't it enough to be baptized and belong to the Church? We've always been told that Filipino Catholics are all Christians. Aren't we? I'm not a bad man. So where does this being 'born again' come into it?"

Carefully Ramon Ilaw and Jim explained what it meant. "You need to make it personal," they said. "Confess to God that you are a sinner; turn from everything that would displease Him and trust in Jesus to forgive you and give you a new heart, washed clean from sin."

A bat skimmed in through the window, circled the room looking for insects and was gone. The buffaloes grunted and scuffled in the shed as they changed position or rubbed themselves against a post. But upstairs no one noticed them. The conversation went on. At last Dading looked Jim and the pastor in the eye and said,

"Well, that's it. I've got it. I believe you. I've known it all my life in a vague sort of way, but you know how they confuse us with penances and absolutions and 'do this' and 'do that'. I can see it all clearly at last. Tell me what to do now and I'll do it."

When Pastor Ilaw had helped him to pray and shown him the words in the Bible, "If anyone is in Christ he is a new creation", they said goodnight.

"We'll come again tomorrow afternoon, shall we? You've got a lot more to learn now."

"Come as often as you can," Dading replied, "There are three hundred people in this *barrio* who need what you've shown me tonight."

Tessie was washing some rice before putting it on to cook. She was puzzled. "What's happened to Dading?" she thought. "It's getting near time for his *mahjong* friends to come and he's taking the table out of his den. And what's he hammering at?" She went through her *sari-sari* store and round to the front of the lean-to. Dading was nailing a plywood board above the door. On it he had carefully painted the words "BAGONG NILALANG"—"A New Creation"!

"Like it?" he asked. But Tessie said nothing and went back to her kitchen.

"What do you say to that?" he said, waving his hand at the sign when Lito and his fishing partner, Pedro, arrived for the evening's game. "New management here. I've sold the *mahjong* pieces and bought a pig! You'll have to go to Sampaguita if you want to play. But sit down a minute. I'll tell you what's happened. You know how black and dirty a *carabao*, a common old water-buffalo, looks when it has been cooling off in a mud-wallow? And how clean and shiny it looks when you wash it down at the river? Well, that's how I feel!"

"Captain Carabao, no less!" said Pedro. "Come off it. Tell us what's up."

"Here, Tessie!" shouted Dading through the wall. "Bring us three bottles of Coke—to celebrate!"

"Coca-cola? Come off it!" Lito said. "Where's your *tuba*?"

Dading led the way into the den. He had brought in more benches and it was all ready for Pastor Ilaw and even a score of neighbours.

"*Barrio* captain goes up the wall," Pedro groaned.

"Sit down. I'll explain," Dading grinned. And when Ramon Ilaw and two of the Sampaguita Christians arrived, Dading, Lito and Pedro were still talking, surrounded by Berting, Pedring, Jun and half a dozen gaping neighbours.

Pastor Ilaw had to go back to the city, but Jim and Betty came often to Santo Domingo. Not only Dading but Lito and now an old man named Mr Madrid and his teenage daughter Chaling were joining them regularly to study the Bible and worship together on Sundays. Tessie and the boys sat with them sometimes, for Dading's sake, but could not make out what was going on; except that Dading and his "New Creation" idea seemed to fit.

One day, some weeks later, Ramon Ilaw paid them another visit. "Hello, it's the *Bagong Nilalang* Chapel now, is it? Praise the Lord!" He was teaching them about prayer. "Why did you folk listen to us and open your hearts to the Lord when we first came here?" he asked. "Because Dading Aranas had heard the Gospel during the war and knew deep down that it is true. Well, yes. But let me tell you something. You all know Juanita, who sells *tuba* in Sampaguita—how she kept on pleading with Judge Sarmiento until he took action for her? Now, God wants us to pray like that, 'without ceasing'. But He isn't unwilling like the judge. He wants to help and promises to answer our prayers. So pray on like Juanita till He does. Be like Jim and Betty here, who prayed for you until you woke up and saw the good things you were missing."

Dading was standing, half leaning against the hollow-block wall which he was building, to turn his den into a chapel. He nodded slowly. Yes, he understood. "I'll have to be like Juanita if Santo Domingo is to become a '*bagong nilalang barrio*' (New Creation village)," he thought.

4 WET NETS AND PRESSURE LAMPS

"Ay . . . isdâ. Ay . . . isdâ. Fish! Fish!" called Floring, walking down the street, beautifully erect, balancing a large round shallow basket of fish on her head. She moved with that curious jerkiness of one who frequently wears wooden clogs and drags them almost without bending the knee.

"Ay . . . isdâ!" she called again and removed her cigarette to spit out some ash. Like so many women she smoked the cheap, brown cigarettes with the lighted end inside her mouth. It was remarkable that in spite of this handicap she could still shout, "Fish", in a loud and relatively clear voice.

Passing Dading's house she heard a prolonged hiss and turned instantly. Filipino ears are permanently tuned for this sound. Do you want to attract someone's attention? Then hiss. Do you want to call a taxi in the middle of a busy street? Just hiss, and the driver will inevitably hear you.

Floring caught sight of Tessie, Dading's wife, beckoning her. Dading's conversion to the *Protestantes* had been a slight on Mother Church, but even to a one-time catechist, business is business, after all. Crossing the street she let down the basket on a bench by Dading's door and removed the large conical rain hat that served a dual purpose in keeping the sun and flies off the fish.

Carefully Tessie made her choice and, as custom and economy required, haggled over the price until she was satisfied. Floring fumbled in the deep pockets of her drab, thick pinafore for the change, thinking to herself, "Tessie's losing weight. And that cough of hers is far worse now. You can't play around with heresy and expect not to suffer for it." And stooping over her basket she surreptitiously crossed herself.

"You must be short of cash since Captain Mahjong packed up his club," she said, standing up.

"Not too bad," Tessie answered, dropping the change into her purse and disregarding the dig at their new way of life. "That only brought him a bit of pocket money. He's found better markets for his coconuts since then. You know, Floring, he may have gone daft over it, but he has given up his vices. And he doesn't lose his temper like he used to. He couldn't be more helpful when my fever comes on, either. Funny stuff, this *Protestante* talk, but you've got to hand it to them, it's not just talk—like our religion?" She flung the final question at Floring with a laugh.

Floring was not amused. Busily taking the cigarette from her mouth she shook the ash off for the umpteenth time and put the glowing stub end back into her mouth.

"How's the net going?" Tessie asked, to change the subject.

"So, so," Floring replied, covering her fish again, ready to go. "At the present rate it will be months before they finish, and it's got to be ready before the *tulingan* shoals get here."

She adjusted the thick coil of cloth that kept the basket balanced on her head. "Attaching the ropes, weights and floats alone takes two weeks on such a big net. It's going to be touch and go, and a lot of hard work. Pedro won't get any real rest for months."

"It'll pay off when the season starts," Tessie said, stifling a cough.

"Hope so," Floring replied; then with a well-practised movement she lifted the basket on to her head again and set off along the street. "Ay . . . isdâ!"

Floring and Pedro lived in the crowded beach area of Santo Domingo where the flimsy homes of the fishermen were huddled together so closely that sometimes their roofs almost touched and there was only enough room to walk between them.

When Floring had set out to sell the fish Pedro had caught in the early hours of that morning, she left him cleaning and repairing his nylon fishing line and its many hooks on the sandy beach. As soon as they were ready and neatly coiled on a wooden frame he went indoors to sleep—in his clothes, lying on a woven palm leaf mat spread out on the bamboo floor. He had to be able to sleep in spite of all the surrounding noise of children crying, dogs barking, the neighbours' radios playing loudly, visitors calling and the flimsy house shaking as if struck by an earthquake whenever anyone moved in it. Somehow he managed to get the rest he needed. This was his life.

Early in the afternoon Pedro awoke. It was hot and sultry.

"Come and have some coffee," Floring said.

He came over just as he was, in his vest and underpants, and sat sleepily on the bench at the table rubbing his chin with its thin straggly growth of a week's beard.

"Look, cornflour cakes and bananas fried in sugar. I thought you would like something tasty. The fish brought a good price this morning. The rough weather kept most of the other men in last night, so fish was scarce and the price was up."

Pedro ate and drank almost in silence. Then, taking his *bolo*, a long, all-purpose knife, he stumped down the bamboo ladder. Squatting on the sand in the shade of his home, he chopped up the fish he had reserved for bait. Even baiting more than a thousand hooks takes a long time, not to mention inspecting and repairing the long line where it shows signs of chafing.

At last, when that was finished, he worked on the net. He and Lito were making it together for the *tulingan* season. It was a mountain of work to get through but during the rainy season the sea was often too rough for them to go out fishing, and when typhoons came it was impossible for days on end to venture out. At these times they squeezed in all the available moments they could on the net, over several months.

Toward sundown the children ran home from school, and Floring had supper ready. Meal times in the *barrios* are for eating rather than conversation and they took no time to consume a large plate of rice with a little fried fish, rounding it off with a banana and a glass of water.

Now all that needed to be done was to fill the pressure lamps, check the engine of the boat and set out to sea.

"Nene!" called Pedro. "Buy the kerosene. Here's the money." His daughter didn't like her father interrupting her game. Pouting peevishly she made off towards the shop with a large bottle in her hand.

"Totoy! You get the petrol." A moment later his son was scuttling through the maze of passage ways among the houses to a garage that supplied the fishing boats.

Finally Pedro emerged from his home carrying his two pressure lamps, fed from a single tank, and his baited line. Totoy came back with the petrol and helped carry an assortment of equipment, a landing net, a basket with food, and his father's *bolo* down to the boat.

Pedro loaded it all in and filled the tank of his small inboard engine. Then with his trousers rolled above the knees he and his son, on either side of the boat, lifted the outspread supports of the wide outriggers and pushed the boat down the slope into the sea.

As soon as it was afloat, Pedro jumped aboard, paddled a few yards to be clear of the shore and, starting the motor, set course for the open sea. A flotilla of other small boats was doing the same, intent like him on spending most of the night bobbing about on the waves.

Pedro pressed his straw hat more firmly down on his head as a gust of wind threatened to remove it. A shower of spray blew across from the splashing outrigger. He reduced speed and wiped his face with the towel he had draped round his shoulders.

"It's going to be cold tonight," he thought, fastening the buttons of his jacket, home-made in battle-dress style out of coarse blue denim. "It'll be good when the *tulingan* arrive and we can fish during the day for a change."

Nearing his favourite fishing ground he could see that several other outrigger canoes were there in a line stretching all along the coast. Some already had their pressure lamps burning.

He stopped his motor, filled the alcohol well of his lamps, pumped up the pressure and lit the lamps with a pop. Carefully he adjusted them so that they shone down into the sea over the side of the boat, and prepared to let out his line.

"What a beautiful sight," exclaimed Betty Evans in the gathering darkness, as she sat with Jim on the beach three miles away at Sampaguita, looking out across the bay. "Look at all those fishing boats! Oh, did you see that one? It has just got its light going. And there's another. There must be scores of them out tonight."

"Those yellowish lights," Jim said, "are the ones on outrigger canoes. They use kerosene pressure lamps. But that one over there," and he pointed further down the coast, "that very bright light must be on a *basnig*. It is a much bigger boat with a generator on board."

"What's the advantage of that?" Betty asked.

"Much brighter lights," Jim replied. "The men in the canoes are not very happy if a *basnig* comes too close to them. The fish are attracted away from the feebler pressure lamps. Then there's real trouble. No fisherman likes to lose his fish."

"How do they actually catch the fish?"

"People like Lito and Pedro use a line with hundreds of baited hooks," Jim explained, "but the *basnig* uses a net. On the *basnig* the crew wait until they can see a great many fish swimming below their lights and then they switch off the lights on one side of the boat, and carefully lower the net deep down on the darkened side, slip it under the fish, and, after waiting a while, pull it up."

"I suppose they catch more that way," Betty commented, skimming a stone over the water.

"Yes, but mostly small fish. The bigger ones are still usually caught in the deep water by the men with a hook and line."

Jim stood up and started to collect together their picnic things. A swim followed by supper on the beach was often the nearest they could get to a day of rest from the incessant blaring of neighbours' radios and people dropping in to have a chat. "How quickly the darkness falls here in the Philippines," he remarked. "We will have to be quick or we won't be able to see our way."

They stood in silence for a moment watching the last deep red flushes of a magnificent sunset fade away. It was breathtakingly beautiful. "Perfect!" murmured Betty. "I wonder if the fishermen stop to look at it? Those nearer lights will be the Sampaguita men. I suppose those further down the coast must be from Santo Domingo."

"Including Pedro and Lito," replied Jim. "If only we could tell which ones they are."

"They are very hard working, aren't they?" she said.

"Yes. And yet Lito manages to come to the Bible studies every Thursday night. It means they're a couple of hours late putting out to sea. Have you noticed, since he was converted he won't miss a meeting for anything? It would cheer him and Dading up no end if Pedro would believe too. He did attend Pastor Ilaw's meetings at first, but Floring put her foot down. It's she who prevents him from coming."

"It is grand to see Lito's enthusiasm as a Christian, isn't it?" added Betty. "He is such a big, tough man too. I'd like to ask him more about fishing."

When they next visited Dading's *Bagong Nilalang* chapel in Santo Domingo, Jim mentioned their interest in fishing.

"You should come with us when the *tulingan* season starts," said Dading with enthusiasm. "That's real fun! You can both go out in our *pukutan*—the boat like a huge outrigger-canoe but not as big as a *basnig*. It has a powerful motor and gets up a good speed."

"Your *pukutan*?" said Jim in surprise. "I didn't know you were involved in fishing as well as everything else."

"Yes, I'm part owner of the new one you've seen on the beach," Dading explained. "Lito and Pedro are the other partners. They have done most of the work building it and making the net, but I have provided the capital."

"When does the *tulingan* season begin?" asked Betty.

"Quite soon now. I'll send a message and you can join us for a day," he answered. "The *tulingan* belong to the tuna family. At this time of the year they come right into the bay in great shoals. I expect you've seen them jumping and splashing and having a great time."

"How do you catch them?" Jim asked.

"It's really quite simple," Dading said. "During the day we go out in the *pukutan* and watch for the fish. When we see them splashing we race to the shoal and surround it with a net."

"It must be a very long net to do that!" exclaimed Betty.

"It is. Ours is 300 fathoms long," he replied, stretching his arms sideways. "And it's four fathoms deep. I'll let you know when to come. You'll see for yourselves."

A couple of weeks later one of Dading's boys arrived with a message and early the next morning Jim and Betty went over to Santo Domingo. Too early, it turned out, for they had a long wait. Still it was a good chance to chat with Dading and the fisherfolk on the beach. They were friendly and interesting. So far the lookout had caught no sign of *tulingan*, and the crew were taking their time.

The net had been draped over long rows of parallel bamboo frames near the beach for drying and repairs. Now it was carefully folded and carried on a bamboo platform to the boat on the shoulders of eight strong men.

With all aboard looking more like pirates than fishermen

the engine was started and the search for *tulingan* began. To protect them from the blazing sun everyone was well covered up, with towels dangling from their wide brimmed straw hats. A look-out stood as high as possible at the prow searching the distance for signs of splashing. But suddenly one of the fishermen relaxing on the engine cover, jumped to his feet shouting, "*Tulingan!*" and pointed down the coast, in the opposite direction. The boat turned in a tight circle, the engine opened up to full speed and spray swept across the after part of the *pukutan* as its outriggers and prow sliced through the choppy water.

"I've never seen anything like it!" shouted Betty into Jim's ear, sheltering now from the spray instead of the sun. "There must be hundreds of fish jumping right out of the sea."

"It looks as though the shoal is heading for shallower water," roared Jim. "It will be interesting to see how they surround them."

Dading joined in. "We are lucky today. You will have to come with us every time, and be our mascots. You bring us good luck!" he shouted above the noise of the racing engine. It had no silencer. "It isn't often that we find them so quickly."

"They are very near the beach!" Jim called.

"Yes, they are," replied Dading. "It is good there isn't a coral reef just here. Our net would get badly torn. This beach is pebbly. The sea is very deep, even close inshore."

Two men took up positions by the long net and as Pedro steered the boat in a tight arc around the shoal, they rhythmically cast fold after fold of the net into the sea.

Lito dropped into the small outrigger canoe they had been towing and slipped its line.

"Look," said Jim. "Lito's taking the rope from the net to the beach."

"And look at all those people running," exclaimed Betty, as along the beach men, women and children appeared as if from nowhere.

As soon as the rope was ashore, everyone grabbed it and started to pull it in. Soon more people arrived and spacing themselves in a long line joined in the work, heaving rhythmically together. Half the volunteers ran further up the beach to start hauling in the other end of the net.

The *pukutan* and the canoe stayed in the deeper water around the net, the crew splashing the sea with paddles to drive the fish towards the beach. The area inside the net was boiling with fish. Men shouted and yodelled in excitement, bringing more opportunists running along the beach to join in.

Glittering fish were being pulled out of the net and thrown up on the beach where they jumped and gasped. Other boats arrived to help carry the catch back to Santo Domingo. The wooden boxes in the boats were soon filled and more *tulingan* were piled on top. All who had helped pull in the net later went home cheerfully carrying a good big fish each.

"I say," said Jim suddenly to Dading, "why did they throw that fish back into the sea?"

Dading laughed. "That's a butete," he replied. "It is poisonous. You can't eat all fish, you know."

"Look at that," Dading exclaimed, hurrying over to pick up a fish. We don't often catch one of these."

"A young shark, isn't it?" suggested Jim.

"It is indeed," said Dading, handing it to him.

"Horrible," said Betty peering at it. "Even when it's so young." Then, wondering whether it was safe to go swimming again she asked, "Are there many sharks here?"

Dading could read her thoughts. "A few," he replied, "but they rarely come so close to land. Our fishermen spend hours in the sea with spearguns and goggles and never seem to be attacked, so it isn't really dangerous."

Dading took the dead shark and threw it into the sea.

"Do you know you are acting out one of Jesus' parables?" Jim asked him.

"Did He ever say something about fish?" Dading replied.

"Yes, quite a lot. For one thing He said that the Kingdom of Heaven is like a net which catches all sorts of fish, good and bad. The fishermen who pull the net ashore are the angels."

"Our fishermen are not exactly angels!" laughed Dading.

"Perhaps not," Jim chuckled. "The end of the world is like the net being pulled in and the Judgment I told you about is the sorting out of the good men and bad. The bad will be thrown into hell."

"How interesting," said Dading. "Then we people of the New Creation are the *tulingan*!"

"Right!" agreed Jim. "It's good that you and Lito and some of the others turned to Christ when you did."

"That's the first time I've heard of fishermen becoming fish," grinned Dading. "I see what you mean. It is all so interesting. The Bible is very close to our lives, isn't it." "Always," said Jim. "Jesus also said, 'Follow Me and I will teach you to fish for men'. So He brings us in both ways. But what are you going to do with your catch now?"

"We'll send them into Sampaguita and if the market there is saturated, we'll cover them with ice and take them straight to the main markets, as far as Manila if necessary."

Dading turned and picked up two *tulingan*. "Here are two that won't be going to Manila," he said with a chuckle. "They're for you. Thanks for your company today. If you roast them whole over charcoal you will find that they are really delicious."

They thanked him and turned to go home, but a moment later Dading ran after them. "By the way," he panted, "I almost forgot to tell you. Berting is graduating from Sampaguita College on Saturday. I hope you'll be there. He is the valedictorian, you know!"

"Congratulations, Dading!" they exclaimed, warmly shaking his hand. "We'll most certainly be there. You must be very pleased. It is an honour that reflects on you too!"

5 THE LONG ROAD TO HAPPINESS

Dading proudly stood his full five feet seven inches, his dignity enhanced by his elaborately-decorated new *barong tagalog* shirt.

"My word, this photo is going to look impressive on our sitting room wall," he thought to himself.

"Now, don't let your teeth show! They will make your skin look dark," echoed in his mind. "Funny how I always remember my father saying that when I was a child."

He pressed his lips together, giving additional severity to his expression. Beside him on the stage, clutching his diploma and perspiring in his unfamiliar dark suit, bow tie, cap and gown stood his younger son, Berting. He too was posing with a very serious expression on his face.

"Ah, if only Tessie could be here now," thought Dading affectionately. "How happy she would be. It is sad so many of our people die of weak lungs. They say TB can be cured. If only we *barrio* folk could afford it." But Tessie was already beyond hope and daily life had to go on. Quickly he banished the thought and concentrated on the photography.

Marcing, the town photographer, fumbled with his ancient Yashica camera. The bulb flashed and the admiring onlookers broke into smiling chatter again.

Berting was tense with suppressed excitement. To be the valedictorian of the Sampaguita College, graduating with a degree in electrical engineering, made him the object of everyone's attention. For his family today was the triumphant climax of four years of common struggle.

From early in the afternoon the "Rizal Sound System" had been playing as loudly as possible a frequently repeated series of scratched, worn-out records of outdated popular songs. The booming loud speakers helped to create a festive atmosphere and draw the townspeople to the stage, impressively crowned with the words, "Sampaguita College. 12th Commencement Exercises."

Chairs had been arranged on the basket-ball court, in front of the outdoor stage, for the students and distinguished guests. The rest of the audience stood, some using cars and jeeps as grandstands.

During the evening an elaborate programme of folk-dances and musical items had entertained the crowd. There was good reason for the college graduation to be regarded as a gala event, a highlight in the calendar of Sampaguita.

The greying Father Areta in his flowing white robes blessed the proceedings and sat prominently on the stage with a paternal smile, applauding the students' efforts.

As valedictorian, Berting had memorized his speech in English. It was freely larded with uncommon words (that made it sound erudite) and although feeling nervous, he managed it well. His father sitting in the audience beamed with pride.

The visiting dignitary for the occasion was Senator Constantino, who possessed to a high degree the ability to speak eloquently about very little for half an hour. He too spoke in English, which most of the audience could not understand. To the surprise of Jim and Betty Evans, many of them chattered freely throughout the tedious speech. It made no difference.

Finally the climax came when Senator Constantino, assisted by the college principal, presented the diplomas and awards. Berting drew the loudest applause, and as he was mounting the steps of the stage, his cousin Rene drew a pistol and fired five shots into the air in his honour.

Berting's older brother, Pedring, stood watching from the edge of the crowd. He would never admit it, but at heart he was jealous of Berting. He himself had neither the aptitude nor the ability for study and had only completed the six years of elementary education. It was not easy to go on working on their farm while his brother enjoyed himself as a student and reaped all the honours.

But now the photographs had been taken, congratulations and handshakes and best wishes from the college staff, fellow students, friends and relations were over, and Berting, luxuriating in his success, made his way home. His arms were full of gaily-wrapped graduation gifts and an escort of neighbours and relatives filled the darkness with banter and laughing.

Dading imagined that Berting, as valedictorian of his college, would quickly find some well-paid employment and soon replenish the family's coffers to enable them to live a little more comfortably after the years of scrimping to pay his college fees. But in this he was disappointed. Berting went frequently to Manila, job-hunting, but jobs were scarce and competition fierce, and having no influential backer he failed to secure work. After numerous disappointments his enthusiasm wore off. Each time he returned home more disillusioned. Increasingly he sat on the balcony of their home whiling away the hours reading tattered magazines and "comics" and often just staring down the hillside, along the narrow road, across the village and out to sea.

His disappointment expressed itself in sullenness and irritability. He became argumentative and restless. He linked up with several other young men idling away the hours at street corners, in gambling dens and restaurants. Often he came home late at night, drunk.

Dading was troubled about his son. One evening after

supper he said to him, "This life of idleness isn't good for you, Berting. You are becoming more cantankerous every day. Why don't you give Pedring a hand tomorrow harvesting the coconuts."

"What?" exploded Berting. "Me, a graduate in engineering, start work in the coconut plantation? Not on your life! What do you think that means?" he demanded, pointing to his framed diploma on the wall. "I didn't do all that study to go out gathering coconuts. What do you think that I am? An uneducated peasant?"

It grieved his father. Hadn't they as a family sacrificed so much to pay for his education? And now he despised them. Even at times when help was urgently needed in the rice fields, Berting wouldn't move a finger to help.

In desperation Dading visited all the influential contacts he knew and even wrote to Senator Constantino to try to secure employment for Berting, but all to no avail. It was a sad anticlimax to all his imagined hopes for a successful career for his son.

One day Berting seemed to be in better spirits. "Glad to see you so much happier today," his father greeted him, as he bounded up the bamboo steps of their house singing one of the latest hit songs.

"Oh, Dad! Felix and I have a great idea. He graduated in engineering with me and we have decided to raise some money to open a shop to sell and repair radios and TV sets and other electrical appliances."

"Where is this shop going to be?" asked his father in surprise.

"In Manila, of course! That's where the money is. When we get this shop going we'll soon earn enough money to set you up in comfort and repay some of the debt I owe you. If we can rally up a few thousand pesos it shouldn't be too long before we get a really flourishing business going."

During the next few days Berting and Felix visited Dr Lopez at the bank, and the more wealthy businessmen and professionals of Sampaguita and Santo Domingo in order to raise the capital needed for this venture.

Not surprisingly no one was willing to hazard his money in a business operated by inexperienced young men.

The frustration and discouragement felt before was nothing compared with the darkness that now descended on him. He disregarded his personal appearance and slouched around with his friends wasting his life in indolence.

Life at home became difficult and joyless for the rest of the family. Berting demanded more money but still would not work on the farm. Bitter arguments erupted between the two brothers.

"There you are, you parasite!" snarled Pedring coming into the house and finding Berting lolling in the rocking chair on the veranda reading a pornographic comic. "Why should I have to slave out my guts to support a louse like you?"

The strain was telling on Dading. Tessie's death had aged him. His Christian friends were supporting him loyally, but Berting's behaviour gave him no let-up. He tried to mediate in his sons' frequent quarrels and bring harmony to their formerly happy home. He looked at the diploma on the wall and regretted that he had encouraged Berting to go to college. The anticipated blessing had turned into a curse.

The bamboo steps creaked as Dading wearily climbed up to the veranda. It was a hot day. He stood and gently fanned himself with his straw hat and gazed down at Berting reclining on a bench, eyes closed, his transistor radio blaring loudly beside him.

"Son, you can't go on like this," he said.

"Why not?" asked Berting impertinently, slowly opening his eyes.

"You are destroying yourself, son," replied his father sadly. "You've lost your self-respect! You don't work. You come home almost every night drunk!"

"Well, find me a job in engineering and I'll work. But I'm not going to work in the fields like a peasant, if that's what you have in mind," retorted Berting.

"You know that I've done all I can to find work for you, Berting," replied his father, sitting down on a sack of rice. "I only wish I knew what else I could do. I'm as disappointed as you."

"Well, you find me the money to set up a shop and I'll make sure that you don't have any more problems," asserted Berting. "All I need is a start, but no one will give me a chance."

"Where am I to find money? We have spent all our money on your education only to land ourselves in this crazy situation," complained Dading bitterly.

"All right! All right! I've heard all that before!" interrupted Berting. "All your sacrifice for your thankless son! Go on. Tell me all again. You had better make a recording to save your breath. You could play it for me all day long and get no end of satisfaction from it."

Dading didn't reply. His son was incorrigible. There was no point in arguing. He would only cause himself more heartache. He sat looking sadly out across Santo Domingo to the almost waveless, sparkling sea. For several minutes neither spoke. Dading was lost in thought. He didn't even notice the radio beating out a new hot tune.

Suddenly Berting sat up. His face had changed. Alert and eager he suggested, "Dad, if we can't borrow money, why don't you give me enough to start the business?"

"But you know we haven't any spare money! I would have done that months ago if we had," sighed his father.

"But you have land!" responded Berting. "Why don't you sell some land? We don't need all our fields."

"We couldn't do that!" replied his father in alarm. "The farm has been in the family for generations and I have worked hard to increase its size. It wouldn't be right to sell part. How would we live anyway?"

"You'd be all right," argued Berting. "There is only you and that idiot Pedring. You wouldn't have so many problems either if you got rid of a few of your scrounging, good-for-nothing workmen."

Dading refused to discuss selling any of his land but in the ensuing weeks Berting persistently repeated his demand. He regarded this as his only possible source of capital.

One day Berting and his father were eating supper together. Dading was gnawing at a chicken drumstick when Berting introduced the now well-worn theme.

"Dad," he said cheerfully. "When are you going to sell off a few fields so that I can have a chance in life? I'm just rotting away here in Santo Domingo. I should be in Manila earning a pile of money. All my education will be wasted unless I use it. After all you have done for my education you wouldn't want it to be wasted, would you?"

Dading gnawed on in silence as though he hadn't heard anything. Then dropping the bone under the table for his patiently-waiting dog, he replied, "You know that we can't break up the farm. I've told you so many times. Why do you keep raising the subject?"

"It's my only hope, Dad," he answered appealingly.

"Oh, something will eventually come. You must be patient!" advised his father.

"How many months have I been waiting already!" retorted Berting. "I'll wait until I'm dead at this rate. You don't have confidence in me or you would do something."

He angrily knocked the cat off the table. There was a burst of snarls and spitting and it fled into a corner.

"Look, Dad," continued Berting with considerable feeling. "One day you are going to die. No! Don't look at me like that! I hope it doesn't happen for a long time, but we must face it, one day it is going to happen. When that day comes Pedring and I will halve the farm. Isn't that right? That will be fine for Pedring because he doesn't know anything except how to grow rice. But I'm not going to be a farmer! Not on my life! What shall I do? Rent out my part to some ignorant tenant? I'd rather sell the land and invest the money in my business. I would gain better interest in that way. Look, why should I have to wait until you die before I can inherit that land? I need it now, not in goodness-knows-how-many years' time. I need it now, not when I'm an old man. Why don't you let me have my share now so that I can start my business, or do I have to drag on year after year like I have during these past months?"

Dading was horrified at the thought. Jumping up he quickly unloaded his mind in a few pungent phrases and stormed into the bedroom where he relieved his feelings by banging about in agitation, unrolling his sleeping mat and hanging his mosquito net.

Berting was not to be deterred. Day after day he pursued his father with this latest idea until in desperation he yielded. Half the farm was sold. Berting was elated.

Everyone knew what was happening. Around the *tuba* stalls in Santo Domingo, half-drunk men discussed this dramatic development until late at night. In loud incoherent voices they argued the rightness of such an act, debating whether this event would bring trouble to their own families should any of their children suddenly demand that their inheritance be given to them immediately. And in many homes anxious men and women denounced their *barrio* captain for yielding to his son's demands.

Sadly Dading rose from his sleeping mat. It was pitch dark and his bleary eyes indicated that he had hardly slept at all. He blew the embers into life, arranged the firewood and soon had the coffee ready.

Their moods were such a contrast. Berting, cheerful, exuberant; his father tearful, morose. In silence they sat at the plain board table drinking sweet, black coffee out of thick white china cups and munching plain tasteless biscuits.

At the sound of a horse and *kalesa* approaching Berting quickly swallowed the remainder of his coffee. They had arranged for Juan, the *tuba* gatherer, to take Berting to Sampaguita in time to catch the 4.30 a.m. bus for Manila.

Saying a brief goodbye to his father, he picked up his *Pan*

Am plastic shoulder bag, quickly descended the creaking steps, climbed into the *kalesa* and was gone.

For a few moments Dading stood on the balcony listening to the fading sound of the horse jogging along the potholed road, then returning to his sleeping mat he spent a sleepless hour until the dawn brought activity to Santo Domingo again.

For months Berting had considered his strategy. He had determined to take as many short cuts as possible to the top. Accordingly he rented pretentious premises in Makati, the fashionable business suburb of Manila, brought in Felix as his assistant, invested in a large American car as a prestige symbol, and determined to make friends with the sons of influential families and forget Santo Domingo.

Dading reeled under the experience. His prayers seemed to go unheard, his faith was shaken and his desire for reading the Bible weakened to vanishing point. Jim Evans and Pastor Ilaw did all they could to help him, but it was Lito's steady friendship that helped him through. "You wait," he kept saying, "everything works out for the best to those who love God. He knows what He is doing. It's a case of seeing how He does it."

Dading knew it was true. With contentious Berting out of the house it was not many weeks before Pedring and his father were back on an even keel. And the Christians in Santo Domingo and Sampaguita prayed steadily for Berting and his father. But Dading had to rely on occasional scraps of news brought back from Manila by friends to learn about his son's activities. He said little and hoped much.

"Your son seems to be making out well in Manila," said the garrulous Celso one day as Dading rode in his *kalesa* from the town to Santo Domingo. "They say he has a marvellous shop in Makati and drives a huge car. Really living it up, he is. Getting right into the social life of the city, they say."

The months sped by quickly and whereas Dading was always eager to hear news of his son, he was not always happy at what he heard. One evening during rice harvest he was leading his *carabao*, pulling a sled loaded with sacks of rice, when Dr Lopez' jeep pulled up beside him. The bank manager was always one for a dig at Dading since he became a Christian. And Berting had put his back up.

"Well, Captain Aranas, it looks as though you are busy," he called to the bare-footed farmer with his trousers rolled up and mud almost to his knees.

Dading wiped the sweat from his face with the small towel wrapped round his head under his broad brimmed hat. "Harvest is always a busy time, sir," he replied respectfully.

"I was at the Araneta Colosseum in Manila watching the heavyweight title match last night," said Lopez.

Dading raised his eyebrows. What was coming?

"Do you know whom I saw there?" continued Dr Lopez. "Berting!"

"Oh, is that so?" replied Dading poker-faced.

"Yes, indeed. He was the smartest eligible bachelor there. He knows how to choose his company too. He was sitting in the ringside seats with senators' and business tycoons' sons. Your son is a very popular young man. I imagine his business must be doing very well."

"I hope so," answered Dading without changing his expression. But the bank manager's look was nothing if not sarcastic.

"Well, I must be on my way. I thought you would like to know the latest," he said, slipping his jeep into gear.

As time passed more and more reports were brought. Unfriendly people made the most of it.

"Pedring, what are you doing out here in the paddy fields? Why don't you go to Manila and live it up with your brother?"

"Dading, your son eats out at the most expensive restaurants in Manila. Why don't you go and join him? Better than rice and dried fish, you know!"

"A proper bumblebee, your brother, Pedring. He is always

in the nightclubs on Roxas Boulevard surrounded by the most attractive hostesses. I wonder that you don't go and have a bit of fun with him—or do you prefer the company of water-buffaloes?"

"I don't know how Berting's business is going. He is always so occupied with his social life. . . ."

After a meeting of *barrio* captains one day, Mayor Abando, back in office after a few years of eclipse by his rival, turned to Dading and asked, "What has happened to Berting?"

"I don't know," replied Dading. "I haven't heard about him for a long time. He never writes to us."

"Well, I don't know anything," explained the mayor, "except that they say his shop in Makati has closed down. I wondered whether he had transferred to some other place or run into problems. The rents are very high there."

Berting had indeed run into problems. He had accumulated enormous debts and with his creditors at his heels had decided to go into hiding. His appeals for help to his wealthy friends had gone unheeded. They merely mocked him for his folly in reaching such a pass.

Eventually Berting found himself in the slums of Tondo, deserted. His misery was intensified by the onset of the rainy season. He erected a miserable, leaking shack of discarded corrugated iron and cardboard cartons. Unsuccessfully he touted for employment.

With his last remaining *pesos* he managed to survive for a few days and then in desperation went to the Dangwa Bus Station. With difficulty he persuaded the *cargadors* to let him also carry passengers' baggage. He would run to meet arriving taxis and buses in the hope of a customer or run out into the street to call a taxi and open its door for a passenger in the hope of a small tip.

He soon lost weight and became dishevelled. He was often hungry and sometimes even begged money for food. Every day became a struggle.

At night in his dingy, dirty shack his mind tortured him by recalling the past. He contemplated suicide but lacked the courage.

The weeks went by and his daily struggle for existence continued without relief. Then one day he felt severe stomach pains. He had dysentery. He was too weak and ill to work. He managed to stagger to a chemist's shop and bought some medicine and returned to his hovel to shiver, often bent double with cramps.

During the next few days his thoughts turned more often to Santo Domingo and his father. "How good to be at home," he said to himself. "Look at this filthy shack! If Dad would have me back, I'd be fed and cared for, but here I'll die. Gosh, how I've sinned and disgraced him. I've wasted all he gave me and brought to him and to myself nothing but shame. But how dare I go home?"

The more he thought, the more he groaned. It was not long before the tears that filled his eyes were falling into the dust on his unswept earth floor. What began as self-pity, slowly changed to the bitterest remorse and from remorse to repentance. "Perhaps he would let me work on the farm," he began to hope. But still he could not face the ignominy of showing his face in Santo Domingo. It did not occur to him that anyone, even his father, would be praying for him. His only hope lay in his father's character. Of that he had no doubts.

Two days later, still terribly weak, he spent his last coins on a little rice which he cooked with plenty of water as a thin gruel, for he was still too sick to take anything more solid.

"What now?" he asked himself, looking at the empty cooking pot. "What now?" No money, no food, nothing! Only memories that haunted him, a conscience that tortured him and not far away, more tears of remorse.

"I'm going home!" he resolved. "If I'm thrown out I'll . . . I'll . . . I'll see what happens first."

The thong of his rubber sandal was broken. He kicked it

off, turned, and without a second look, left the hovel and stumbled towards the bus station.

The open-sided bus already had its engine running and was almost full of passengers. He climbed on board. His neighbour gave him an unwelcoming glance as he, dishevelled, dirty, bare-foot and emaciated, sat on the bench seat.

Vendors were shouting their warès: maize, peanuts, bread, rice cakes, oranges. The conductor climbed on to the bus and tapped the roof with his ticket punch; the driver revved the engine and drove on to the highway.

Soon they left behind the traffic-clogged streets of Manila and sped down the straight cemented country road. The early morning breeze in the open bus was pleasant and refreshing.

After travelling several miles the conductor scrambled along the outside of the bus (the space inside was too valuable for a passage way), asking the passengers for their destinations.

"Where are you going?" he asked Berting.

"Sampaguita," he replied.

A few minutes later the conductor, holding on to the roof supports, made his way along the outside again handing the passengers their tickets. If he could not hold each passenger's reply unfailingly in his head until he had punched each ticket, he would not dare to be a conductor. It was a matter of professional pride.

The bus raced on through the plain of rice paddies, across hills covered with sugar-cane fields, coconut and citrus fruit plantations, through villages and towns. From time to time during the two hours or more the conductor collected fares from passengers nearing their destination. (Who would pay for something he had not yet received?)

Several miles from Sampaguita, he came to collect Berting's fare. Berting had been waiting for this moment, anticipating it ever since he left his shack. Accordingly he had been pretending to be asleep for most of the journey. Now his neighbour was nudging him, trying to rouse him, but he did not respond immediately. The longer he could delay the dreaded moment, the further the bus would take him.

Finally he was obliged to "waken" and blankly looked around.

"Your fare!" demanded the conductor.

"Whose?" asked Berting sleepily.

"Yours!" said the irritated conductor with suitable emphasis.

"But it is still a long way to go," replied Berting shutting his eyes again. "I'll pay you at the proper time."

The conductor was not to be deterred. "I want your fare now," he insisted, staring pointedly at Berting's tatters.

Berting slowly fumbled through his pockets one by one. Delay meant more miles. The conductor watched the performance with increasing realization of what he suspected from Berting's appearance.

"I'm sorry," said Berting eventually with feigned agony and surprise, "I can't find it. I must have lost it. I've been pick-pocketed!"

"You had better pay!" shouted the conductor angrily banging the roof with his ticket punch and shouting "*Para!*" "Stop!" The driver looked in surprise through the long mirror over his head. Why stop out on the open road among fields?

"This passenger refuses to pay!" roared the conductor.

The bus stopped and Berting, in great embarrassment, got off. So did the conductor and driver.

Berting apologized profusely. The conductor cursed him and snatched back his ticket. There was little else they could do. After giving him a thorough tongue-lashing the driver climbed back into his seat, and started up. With all the other passengers scowling and the conductor's torrents of abuse continuing unabated, the bus disappeared in a cloud of fumes.

Berting stood in the shade of a large mahogany tree licking

his psychological wounds and congratulating himself on getting safely so far.

A passenger jeepney came in sight. He signalled it to stop and climbed in at the back.

Arriving at the road junction for Santo Domingo, at the outskirts of Sampaguita, he hissed to stop the jeepney and got out.

"Hey!" shouted the jeepney driver angrily backing his jeepney to Berting who was walking away. "Where is your fare?"

"Oh, I'm very sorry," said Berting affably. "Didn't I pay? My mind was on my business. I'm so sorry."

The driver, thoroughly roused, jumped out of his jeepney and advanced on Berting with clenched fists. "Pay up!" he shouted and thumped Berting on the chest. This was more than Berting had reckoned on, so, shaken and trembling, he apologized profusely, dragging out the time as long as he could. Sure enough, the other passengers became restless, wanting to finish their journey, and seeing that there was no hope of recovering the fare, the driver cursed Berting roundly and, still shouting abuse, climbed back into his jeepney. To give vent to his anger he accelerated rapidly and shot off down the road.

Berting looked at the familiar scene and remembered the last time he had been there. It jolted him out of his slum-rat mentality and he blushed at the memory of his past. At least no one on the jeep had recognized him. Now to face his father and take whatever was coming to him.

Weak and dejected, he could only walk slowly with frequent rests down the three-mile lane to Santo Domingo. By this time it was roasting hot midday and most people were having their *siesta*, drowsing on their bed-mats or rocking gently to and fro in a hammock. He was glad that hardly anyone saw him as he skirted the village.

Then he caught sight of the palm-thatched roof of his old home. Tears came to his eyes. Shame welled up in his heart.

"What now?" he wondered. He dared to hope, but could scarcely control his trembling.

He started the slow ascent. There was movement. Someone was coming down the steps of the house and running towards him. "It looks like Dad," he thought, "but he hasn't run like that for years. Is he coming to drive me away?" He stood fearing the worst.

He could never accurately remember what happened next. The welcome was so overwhelming. His father embraced him breathlessly. "Welcome home, son," he panted. "I've been waiting so long for you. I've almost worn out the old rocking chair waiting for you."

It was too much. "I'm sorry, Dad," sobbed Berting. "I'm such a sinner. Such a disgrace. I'm ashamed of myself. I'm sorry for all I've done. I don't deserve to be your son."

The dog chained to one of the house stilts jumped up to lick his hand. The neighbours appeared, beaming their pleasure. Dading led him indoors and quickly put on a meal to refresh him.

"You are dusty and tired after the journey," he said. "There's water in the butt. Have a shower while I make some coffee. And I'll find a change of clothes for you."

"Rene!" he called to his nephew. "Get out the *barong tagalog* for me; the one I wore at Berting's graduation. I haven't worn it since. He shall have it to welcome him home. And the shoes Berting left when he went to Manila. They are on top of the wardrobe." And to the children from nearby who had come to share the excitement, "Benito, call your father and Berting's uncle Leon. Ask them to kill my pig and to roast it whole. Quickly now! Run!"

"Now call your parents, Rene; ask them if they'll organize the cooking and kill the brown goat."

"You boys, catch some hens—and the rooster!"

Producing some money from his pocket he called his niece Lydia. "Quickly, go and buy tomatoes, garlic, lard and ginger roots. We are going to have a real feast tonight. We'll make it a surprise for Pedring. He deserves a celebration too. Tell everyone to bring their guitars. We are going to have the biggest feast Santo Domingo has seen for years!"

Pedring was out on the farm. He sheltered from the midday sun beneath a spreading acacia tree and went on weeding all through the afternoon. Then he stood and stretched his aching back. "Bless me, the sun is sinking," he said to himself. "I must be heading home." His legs felt stiff after crouching all day, up to the calves in water, weeding the rice paddies, and he looked forward to a good supper and an early night's rest.

Passing by the pasture field he checked to see that the *carabaos* were safely tethered by their wallows. Clouds of gnats danced in the twilight above the pools of well stirred mud where all that was visible of the immersed *carabaos* were their enormous horns, twitching ears, dilating nostrils and large passive eyes.

Nearing home he was surprised to hear music coming over loudspeakers. Then he noticed the whole surroundings of his home had changed. A great awning of palm leaves had been constructed on to the side of the house as if for a wedding feast. Neighbours and relations were busily hurrying to and fro. The smoke from several fires under the great mango tree in the yard was slowly curling upwards.

"What's this?" he wondered. "What's happened? Has father died?" He wanted to run to find out, but anxiety held him back. He stood wondering.

He was startled when Leon's wife Maria came hurrying past on the path below him carrying a heavy basket of plates, glasses, forks and spoons.

"Auntie!" he called after her, "what's happening?"

"Why, your brother has come home! Didn't you know?" she replied, pausing to rest the basket on a convenient log. "Isn't it wonderful! Your father is so happy. The pig is being barbecued. You never saw such a feast in all your life. Everyone is coming."

"Well, I'm not!" he replied angrily. "And you can tell Dad so, if you like."

Dading was beaming with joy, directing the arrangements of a score of planks on trestles to make a long table when he was interrupted by Maria.

Noticing her troubled expression he said jovially, "What's bothering you, Maria? Taken on too much? This is no time for sadness. Come on, join in the fun and forget your worries!"

"Oh, Dading," she replied. "Pedring is out by the jackfruit tree and seems all upset. I think you had better go and talk with him."

For a moment a cloud passed over Dading's face. "I will indeed," he said graciously. Turning to his helpers he excused himself, "Carry on, I'll be back in a moment."

It was almost dark now but Dading could just discern the figure of Pedring standing under the tree.

"Ah, there you are, Pedring," he called with forced cheerfulness. "Come and join the celebration. Berting has come home and we are giving him a real welcome. We've been waiting for you. Berting is asking for you."

"Think I'm coming in?" snarled Pedring.

"Why not?" enquired his father anxiously.

"I'm not going to welcome home that filthy animal. I wouldn't defile my mouth by calling him my brother!" He spat the words out with bitterness.

"But Pedring, he is your brother. It is only right that we should be happy now that he has come home. It has been almost as though he were dead," reasoned his father.

"Happy?" retorted Pedring. "Anyone would think that the President of the Philippines had arrived by all this celebration you have laid on. I'm disgusted! Here I am, I've worked for you here all my life, from dawn till dark every day. When did you ever roast a pig for me? When did you ever get the Rizal Sound System for me? Come on. Answer that! I just don't count in your reckoning."

"But Pedring," started Dading, only to be cut short by another angry torrent.

" . . . and here this poisonous snake has the face to come back, this wastrel who talked you into giving him half the farm. You always give in to him and try to please him. Now after he has thrown away your money on prostitutes you welcome him back with a feast. See what honours you shower on this debauched fool! When did he last do a day's work? Who slaved to pay his fees when he was in college? Now see how he has turned out. And you give him a feast!" Pedring's voice rose in frenzy till it broke and he stamped his foot like a child. Jealousy and bitterness overwhelmed him.

There was almost a sob in his father's voice as he answered. "Pedring! It's true that you have always been with me. Berting's return home isn't going to affect your inheritance. Don't fear that. All that remains is yours. You know that. But it's only right that we should be happy and celebrate his return. It's a feast for all of us, for you as much as him. He's been far away for so long, but now he has come back. He has left his wicked life. His new life begins today. He has genuinely repented. You will find him completely changed."

"He had better be!" interjected Pedring, calming his voice again.

"Pedring," continued his father. "Shouldn't we be like God who loves us and receives us when we repent of our sins and turn to Him? Come now. Come into the house. Join the feast and be glad, as God is, for the return of your brother."

"God!" said Pedring. "Always God!" But he followed Dading back to the house.

6 TYPHOON OVER SANTO DOMINGO

Captain Mahjong put on his sunglasses and straw hat and climbed down his steep front steps. As his house was built so high on stilts he always came down carefully. With Berting's return from Manila, Dading had found a new zest for life. He radiated happiness and looked several years younger than his greying hair indicated.

He cast an encouraging smile at the fishermen preparing their lines for the night's fishing.

"Late moon tonight," he said. "Should be good fishing."

"Yes," they grunted and continued baiting their scores of hooks with pieces of fish.

"That is a fine boat Pedro and Lito have built for you," Dading went on.

"They're good boat builders," replied one of the fishermen. "But have you seen what Pedro is building now?"

"No, what?"

"He is building himself a house!"

"Not before it was needed either," said Dading. As *barrio* captain he had been getting concerned for Pedro's family. "Some of the houses in Santo Domingo could do with some rebuilding."

"I must walk along and see what Pedro's doing," he mused. "Funny how Pedro is better at building boats than houses. Perhaps because he's all fisherman and not a landsman. But in this uncertain life of ours a man needs to be able to farm and fish and turn his hand to a craft like carpentry. Times are always hard, it seems, and most of us have such large families to support." Dading's thoughts wandered. "It feels as if my own family is growing more than any, with so many of us becoming Christians. But that's nothing to complain of. If only my boys were part of that family."

Dading walked westwards, wandering in and out among the crowded houses along the sea front. The sound of hammering came from the far end and soon he caught sight of Pedro high up in the framework of his house, balancing on a cross beam and clenching a long nail between his teeth. Dading's experienced eye summed up the construction of the building. The four corner posts were already embedded in concrete blocks which themselves lay well embedded in the sand.

"You haven't wasted any time," he called out in greeting. "But why are you building so far in front of the other houses?"

"It was the only available site I could find," said Pedro. "But it really will be most convenient. When I beach my boat in the early morning I'll only have to pull it a little way up for it to lie safely under my house. As for my fish, I'll simply have to throw them to my wife on the balcony and we'll have fresh fish for breakfast in no time."

Dading only grunted.

Pedro went on banging away vigorously, thinking happy thoughts in a small world of his own.

"Oh well . . . Time for supper, I suppose," thought Dading. "No good trying to change Pedro's mind." And he retraced his steps homeward. In imagination he could already smell the *tulingan* spitted on a stick, sizzling over a charcoal fire and the rice steaming in its pot. "After supper I'll enjoy a chat with old man Madrid. Hope he drops in as he promised."

As Dading sat on a rickety bamboo bench outside his house in the cool of the evening his neighbour Ramon looked out of his window and remarked to him, "They tell me Lito's building a new house up on the hill."

"Yes," said Dading. "And Pedro's building on the beach. I watched him at it this afternoon."

Ramon missed the point that Captain Mahjong would have liked to discuss Pedro's home with him and not to be outdone he said, "I heard that Lito's wife kept nagging him till he gave in. She kept on about the rainy season approaching and how during last year's typhoons their house had leaked like a sieve. She reminded Lito that he had had to pin the house down with heavy wire, like the guy ropes of a tent, to keep it from being blown right away. How our fish wives can carry on! Myrna's no exception!"

"Some of them have tongues like hacksaws," remarked Dading with a wink, "But have you noticed how Myrna has changed recently?"

"Yes, since Lito agreed to rebuild!" Ramon said. "But although he started yesterday morning, he has only one corner post in position so far."

"Why so slow?" Dading asked.

"Well, since he decided to build on the hill, he has so much rock to dig into and further to walk from the sea," replied Ramon. "And he will have to leave his boat a long way from his house. It'll be difficult to look after it from away up there. Lito's a blockhead! What's more, he talks about cool breezes on the hill. Cool breezes!"

"Hmm, indeed!" remarked Dading slowly, thinking to himself. "But Lito usually knows what he's up to."

"Besides, the artesian well on the hill keeps breaking down," Ramon went on. "It's no place to build a house!"

"Ah, Brother Madrid!" Dading called out in welcome. And shuffling along the bench to make more room he added, "Chaling too! Come along."

"Thank you, Captain," Chaling answered, "but I'm on my

way to Mrs Cruz. We're doing a Bible correspondence course together. Did you know?"

Old Mr Madrid sat down, and while the evening star grew brighter and the bats circled, Dading and he discussed the development of the little church in Santo Domingo.

A few days later, Dading looked at his watch. "It's about time I went to the *barrio* council meeting," he thought.

As he passed along the sea front he was surprised to note Pedro's progress. It was truly remarkable. Pedro was actually sitting on the new split-bamboo floor of his balcony, busily mending his fishing net. The paddle of his canoe was propped up beside him ready for fishing.

Dading placed his large veined hand around one of the corner posts and gave it a tug. It seemed steady enough. He closely examined the coconut leaf shingles of the house, gazing up at them from beneath. The best bamboo is cut after Christmas.

"It's April and your bamboo looks fresh," remarked Dading, puzzled. "Did you soak it in the sea for a few days to discourage the woodborers?"

"Couldn't wait," said Pedro. "I had to get it finished. There's so much to do."

Dading hurried on. The meeting of village councillors was being held to discuss the government's new irrigation scheme, to improve the supply of water to the paddy fields.

After the meeting the councillor who represented the hill area turned to Captain Mahjong as they drank a glass of black coffee together and said, "You know Lito is building a house on our hill? Would you believe it, he has been working all day for several days and as I passed this morning he was only just finishing the framework of the roof. He's so slow that no one will employ him to build a house unless he's paid by the job and not by the day!"

Dading half shut his eyes and thought deeply. "All the same, he's the carpenter people go for if they can," he said, half to himself.

Eventually Lito finished his house on the hill. His wife had polished the split-bamboo floor with floor-wax, using half a coconut husk to shine it. A gaily painted "God bless our home" was hung above the entrance way.

As Myrna fed the noisy pig, tied in its place under the new house, she thought of her husband. At last he was free to go fishing with his partner Pedro. There would be fish again for the family. Their diet would be less simple. She paused and looked lovingly out in the direction of the sea. "Who'd have thought it?" she laughed. "My drunken *tuba* addict turning into a saint! Where's that Bible? I must steal another look at it while he's out."

As she turned she noticed the wind rustling in the trees. The sky had been sullenly overcast and now black clouds were coming closer.

"The west wind means rain," she thought.

Sure enough, after that brief warning the tropical rain began to fall in large drops, bouncing in thousands of three-inch fountains on the beaten earth.

Her mind turned to Lito again.

Out at sea in their outrigger canoe Lito and Pedro also noticed the dark clouds building up.

"We haven't caught much but we'd better hurry home," said Lito. "God help us if it's a freak typhoon! They blow up so quickly during this season."

Lito and Pedro paddled hard for the land. The wind was now blowing strongly. The rain began to lash their faces. Waves broke over the prow. Both were drenched to the skin. Pedro baled water from the bottom of the boat. Other canoes were also racing for safety.

The storm churned the sea into a foaming whiteness. Soon Pedro and Lito began to despair of ever reaching the shore alive. In silence they urged the canoe homewards, unspoken fears driving them to the limit of their strength. Time seemed to stand still. They paddled on blindly. At last they could see more clearly through the rain. White breakers were roaring and dashing high up on to the beach. They steadied their canoe to ride the crest of a giant wave. There was a sudden acceleration. They were swept forward. With a jolt and a crunch they hit the sand. Instantly they leaped out to seize the outrigger and heave the boat high up on the beach against the strong undertow of the wave as it receded.

"Thank God!" exclaimed Lito. "We are safe. I thought we would never make it!"

Pedro glanced at the row of houses fringing the beach. The waves were crashing dangerously close to them. Then through his dripping hair he took a closer look at his own new home. He could not believe his eyes. The corner posts were leaning and the balcony was all askew.

Pedro called out in alarm to his wife, Floring. There was no answer. The rain pelted down. The wind howled. The sky looked like lead. At last his wife called from a neighbour's house, "Our house was collapsing. We had to take refuge here."

"At least you're safe," shouted Pedro through the storm.

"Lito, help me shore up my house before it is too late."

Lito's first thought had been to make straight for his own home, but he loyally helped his friend. With bamboo poles left around from the building the two propped up the leaning corner posts and balcony. All the time the storm was increasing in fury.

When Lito could help no more he hurried home to his house on the hill.

Myrna had sensibly battened down the palm leaf shingle windows. His two youngest children, naked, had been enjoying the rain outside as it poured from the edge of the roof, but as the storm grew worse she called them in and dressed them. As soon as she had realized that a typhoon was coming she resourcefully boiled an enormous pot of rice. Beside it she put a large truss of bananas spiralling on their stem. Typhoon diet! In such a wind it was impossible to keep a fire going. Glad that she had nagged Lito till he built them this house, and thankful that the roof did not leak, she kept looking down the hill until he appeared. He changed his sodden clothes and then there was nothing more they could do. The whole family huddled together to keep warm and snatched what sleep they could in all the noise and shuddering of the storm. Exhausted, Lito dropped off even before the children, but Myrna could not sleep. She realized how grateful she was, most of all for his safety.

On the third day of the typhoon Dading looked out from his window to a slightly brighter sky. The wind had dropped. He saw the *barrio* women carrying black umbrellas and squelching in wooden clogs through the thick mud. Children were playing together, delighted to escape from indoors again, and glad of the unexpected holiday from school.

Dading gazed across the fields and sadly noted that most of the banana plants and many trees had been uprooted.

"I'd better go and inspect the storm damage," he said aloud.

Someone passed by and shouted that the pump on the hill was not working at all now, but he couldn't catch all that was said.

"I'll go and see for myself. If people drink unclean water we may be in for a cholera epidemic," he thought.

As Dading struggled up the hill to the artesian well, he saw several women spreading out sheets and clothing on low bushes and on a wire fence. At last the sun was trying to break through. Almost everything in every home had been drenched. There was a lot of drying to be done.

He made a mental note. "I judged correctly. Lito is the good workman I always believed him to be. That house will last for fifty years. And its foundations are planted firmly into the rock."

Dading put men on repairing the pump immediately.

On his way home again he greeted his fellow-villagers. "I can't remember a typhoon like this for thirty years." The sun was warming everyone's spirits.

Then he passed on to the part of the village near the beach, between the crowded houses, down the narrow alleyways he went. "Terrible damage this storm has done to our *barrio*!" he noted with concern.

Suddenly, what a sight met his eyes!

Pedro, utterly dejected, sat on the broken steps of his new home surveying the damage. His house had collapsed. The concrete corner blocks themselves had been undermined by the waves. The posts had fallen. The woven bamboo walls were sodden with rain and sea-spray. Pedro's children sat huddled together on a neighbour's veranda.

Dading bent over and picked up some sand. He did not need to speak. The action was all the advice Pedro needed. He looked at Pedro and said, "We'll give you a hand as soon as the soil dries out a bit, Pedro."

Pedro nodded. "I gambled on it, Captain," he said.

Dading's eyes twinkled. "Why not rebuild up on the hill near Lito," he said. "You'll have a good foundation there. If you like I'll help you find a site."

Pedro gratefully agreed.

"I'll tell my sons," Dading went on. "I'm sure Pedring and Berting will lend a hand to carry whatever you can salvage from here. You can count on Lito and some other men in our church too. If you approve I'll have a word with them tonight."

Pedro's face brightened. "At least I know when my luck's in," he said.

"By the way," Dading went on. "You do know you are always welcome to come in on our meetings, don't you? A few years ago you used to come to the Bible studies in my lean-to, if I'm not mistaken."

Pedro tossed his head in the direction of his neighbour's house, where his wife was husking the floor slats. "Yes, but you know Floring. Her past as a catechist dies hard. She didn't like me attending, so for a quiet life I stopped. But I'm interested in your religion. Lito talks about it while we're fishing."

Dading surveyed the ruins of Pedro's house again. "Well, whatever Floring thinks, you'll have to decide for yourself which foundation you are going to build your own life on," he said. "Ask Lito. He knew what he was doing when he chose Jesus instead of superstition."

But Pedro wasn't the only one with a major problem that day. Not far away from Pedro's ruined house, Juan, the amiable *kalesa* driver, was coming to a decision as he drove laboriously through the muddy streets. Time was running out. It was imperative to find a solution. He decided he would take action the very next day, Sunday. A plan had formed in his mind!

7   BOOMERANG

It was Sunday morning in Santo Domingo. Juan was clomping around in his wooden clogs in the mud left by the typhoon, feeding and harnessing his scrawny horse, and sprucing up his rickety *kalesa*.

The hens, awakened by his intrusion, watched from their bamboo perch with blinking eyes and jerky head movements. Concluding that a new day had begun, one by one they fluttered to the ground, stretched, flapped their wings and, clucking, started to scratch and peck around the house in search of food.

The cockbird roosting on the roof stood, stretched himself, surveyed the yard in the slowly increasing light and crowed lustily. Haughtily cocking his head, he listened to the reply of a distant rooster, and then noisily flew down to strut among his harem.

"Now I'll get ready," thought Juan, slipping his feet out of his clogs at the foot of the rickety bamboo steps of his flimsy palm leaf house. It was convenient living up on stilts. The underneath had been readily adapted as a stable.

As he climbed up he hardly noticed his youngest son Kiko sitting halfway up the steps hugging himself in the cool morning air. Kiko was watching the sun rise and as its rays began to feel warm, so his sleepiness evaporated.

At the stove Juan's wife, Rosa, tried to start the wood fire by gently blowing the embers. The pleasant ritual of a hot cup of well-sweetened black coffee started every day.

Juan crossed the sleeping mats to find his trousers and best shirt. They were suspended on a hanger from a piece of rattan in the corner of the one-roomed house.

Maria, his fifteen-year-old daughter, quickly and noiselessly stacked the family's pillows, folded the sheets and mosquito nets and rolled up the sleeping mats.

His well-built, handsome son Ricky sat dreamily leaning against the bamboo supports of the wall as if reluctant to start his chores—carrying water from the distant pump.

Juan dressed, descended the steps and harnessed his horse into the *kalesa*.

"Aren't you going to drink some coffee before you go?" enquired Rosa.

"No, I'll not be long!" replied Juan, for his secret resolution came first.

A flick of the whip and the horse started for town. At a steady trot the high-wheeled *kalesa* swayed rhythmically, mainly the effect of a strained axle caused by over-loading.

The morning air was cool and invigorating, but Juan noticed little. He was lost in thought about his plans and hopes for the day.

As though by instinct the *kalesa* halted. Aling Lilia and her two teenage daughters climbed up the awkward steps into the *kalesa*. She had a devotion to Saint Anthony and accordingly dressed in the chocolate brown habit of his order. Only illness prevented her from hearing mass daily.

Not a word was spoken on the journey or as she paid their fare at the large, imposing entrance of the Roman Catholic church facing the town *plaza* of Sampaguita.

Silently the church was filling and worshippers knelt reciting their prayers, awaiting the commencement of the mass. Juan, self-consciously, for it was unusual for him to attend church, found a seat in a back pew. Today was an important day and every detail must be observed carefully to ensure the help of the Almighty.

Juan remained seated after the mass. With an expressionless face he gazed at the altar apparently oblivious of the departing congregation.

He ignored the glances of the self-righteous which seemed to say, "I'm surprised to see you here this morning. I hope you are going to reform! And after all the things you've said about Father Areta and the church!"

At last he alone remained. He slipped out of the pew. Silently and with great deliberation he walked to the front of the church and knelt before the high altar. With great earnestness he prayed, "Oh, Blessed Virgin, have mercy upon me and help me. Holy Mother, you know that my son Ricky is to be married on Wednesday and I haven't any money for a feast. Already I have so many debts I don't know what to do. Lady Mary, I will take my best fighting cock to the cockpit this afternoon. Please ensure that I win so that I can buy a pig for the feast. Holy Mother, I'll light a candle for you here every day for a month if you help my cock to win. Amen."

Feeling greatly relieved and already sensing the success that now awaited him Juan left the church, briskly climbed into his *kalesa*, flicked his whip at his patiently-waiting horse, and cheerfully drove home.

By the time he arrived Kiko had removed the fighting cocks from their cages under the house and pegged them out around the yard out of range of each other with a string attached to one leg.

After a breakfast of boiled rice, fried eggs and coffee, Juan examined his cocks carefully, especially the Texan on which his hopes rested. Squatting on his haunches he caressed it and stroked its feathers. He blew cigarette smoke under its wings and in its face. He damped its feathers with water to make it unafraid of being wet with blood, and he murmured, "You're going to fight today, and you've got to win! You must win the money for Ricky's wedding feast!"

Lunch over, Juan, feeling confident of the efficacy of his prayer to the Virgin, and sporting his best straw hat, made off for the cockpit with the Texan under his arm and all the family's money in his pocket.

From a window Rosa watched his departure, her anxious face betraying her premonition.

The open-sided cockpit was crowded with men sitting on tiers of seats surrounding the vital arena. There was a continual murmur of a hundred conversations which suddenly reached a crescendo of shouting when a fight was taking place. The air was tense, the betting heavy. Large sums of money were being won—and lost.

During an interval Juan was approached by the formidable, cigar-chomping bank manager Dr Lopez. He struck an imposing figure, surrounded by his henchmen and with a ·45 pistol as a status symbol stuck prominently in his expansive belt.

"They say you have a fine bird today," he said affably in the guttural voice of a man given to alcohol and tobacco. "Let me see it."

He took Juan's Texan in his flabby hands and stroked the cock critically with his tubby fingers. Removing his sunglasses he examined it more closely. "Hmm, not bad at all. Are you going to fight it today? Put it up against mine!"

Juan examined Dr Lopez's red rooster carefully. Dr Lopez was an expert at cockfighting. He took his best birds to Manila and gambled heavily on them there. "Only his inferior birds are fought here in Sampaguita," thought Juan. "Perhaps my Texan can beat this one."

Realizing that a fight with one of Dr Lopez's cocks would encourage heavy betting, and being flattered by the sudden prominence this would achieve for him, Juan accepted the challenge.

There was a murmur of excited voices as the "christ" of the cockpit, the middleman through whom bets are placed, took the bets. Juan, flushed with excitement, put all his money on his cock. "The Texan is strong and will fight well," he convinced himself. "The Virgin Mary will answer my prayers. It is going to win!"

Razor-sharp spurs were attached to the cocks' feet. Now they were ready to fight. First they were introduced to each other. Their hackles rose like Elizabethan ruffs as they stared angrily into each other's face. Suddenly the fight erupted. Wings flapping, feet kicking, blades flashing, they flew at each other, stabbing, pecking, feathers flying. The crowd stood shouting and cheering, urging the cocks on.

Blotches of red quickly appeared where wounds had been inflicted. The frantic pace of the fight lessened. The cocks paused, panting, heads extended horizontally glaring at each other.

Another blurred flurry of feathers and another pause. The Texan made a feeble attempt to continue the fight and then it tottered and fell mortally wounded.

The winning cock tried to crow its victory but only managed a weak gurgle, then it too collapsed and feebly kicked as it tried to stand again.

Juan stared in disbelief. His rooster had lost! It couldn't be! The Virgin had failed him! His hopes were crushed; his money gone.

Clutching his dead Texan by the legs, in a daze of despair he stumbled out of the cockpit and with intensifying agony of spirit made his way home.

Rosa saw him coming, his hunched shoulders, the dangling dead cock, not even wrapped in newspaper to conceal the defeat from the neighbours. As he slowly climbed the uneven steps her sobs indicated plainly that she realized what had happened.

In silence they sat. There was nothing to say. By his foolishness disaster had overwhelmed them. In silence Rosa kindled the fire again, her tears running slowly down her hollow cheeks. With a pan of boiling water she scalded the feathers of the dead bird and began plucking.

That evening a joyless family gathered to eat fried chicken, a not infrequent Sunday evening dish in their home, the long silences broken from time to time by irritable outbursts from one or another.

Later that night as the smoking cloth wick of the kerosene bottle lamp threw eerie shadows on the walls of their dingy room, Ricky and his father had a stand-up row.

"You idiot! You fool! I'm ashamed to call you my father," Ricky shouted in anger. "You've thrown away all our money. If Virgie and I can't have a feast on Wednesday we'll elope and get married before the Judge!" He spat vigorously out of the window to give added emphasis to his determination.

A shrunken old man now, Juan squatted on the floor pleading his good intentions. "Blame the Virgin!" he retorted. "She let me down! I'll never pray to her again, or go inside that church again until I'm carried there in a coffin!"

Tempers flared, the dispute grew hotter until Ricky, shouting abuse at his father, stumbled down the steps of their home and disappeared into the night.

Silence descended. The rooster on the roof shuffled and subsided again. The neighbours turned over on their hand-woven palm leaf sleeping mats and gratefully settled down to sleep at last.

Next morning several peasants in creased, ill-fitting clothes were sitting on the bench inside the Sampaguita Rural Bank. Their expressionless faces turned to see the latest arrival. A silent Juan joined them.

When the manager's chic little clerk enquired his business Juan would say nothing except that he must see Dr Lopez. And when the girl informed him with an air of superiority that Dr Lopez was exceedingly busy and that he would have to wait a considerable time, Juan did not reply. As a poor man he was used to this kind of treatment.

Juan felt chilled as his perspiration dried in the air-conditioned bank. It was already hot outside but in here the air was refreshingly cool. He had only been inside the bank once before and so he glanced round, cautiously observing every detail.

Eventually his turn came. He was ushered into the bank manager's office. He felt ill at ease and out of place in the well appointed room. Humbly standing by the door he nervously fingered the wide brim of his straw hat.

"Oh, it's you, Juan," gruffly commented Dr Lopez as he looked up from his desk. A large diamond ring glittered on his hand as he indicated a chair. "Sit down," he commanded. "What do you want?" the same abrasive voice demanded brusquely. Gone was the affability of yesterday. His elaborately decorated *barong tagalog* shirt lent him dignity and enhanced the impression he wished to give of authority and power.

Sitting anxiously on the edge of the chair Juan poured out his woes. All his hopes and money had been lost yesterday at the cockpit. Ricky was to be married, and he needed money for the feast on Wednesday. Could he please borrow just five hundred *pesos*. He would repay them as soon as possible.

"So you want your money back with interest, is that it?" replied Dr Lopez with a sly grimace. "Good gracious, man, you can't have a loan from a bank for a feast!"

Juan pleaded with him. "There's no one else who can help me," he declared pathetically. Dr Lopez finally agreed to a private loan—on condition that Juan paid fifty *pesos* a month interest on the loan until it was repaid.

Juan could do nothing but accept the outrageous terms. "And you had better be prompt with your payments, Juan, or you will be in trouble," threatened the bank manager.

The glittering hand indicated the door and Juan, the money in his pocket, found himself out of the artificial coolness and into the humid heat of the familiar street where he felt more secure.

As he jogged along in his *kalesa* seeking passengers the tension within him slowly relaxed. "I'll have to work very hard now to pay off this debt," he decided. "But tomorrow is another day. I'll worry about that later."

The months passed and Juan fell further and further behind in his payments. His debt was building up instead of being paid off. Ricky could find only occasional seasonal employment and Virgie was now expecting a baby. All living together brought an additional drain on Juan's meagre earnings. He was driving his poor emaciated pony to its limit these days to earn all he could.

It was high noon and the sun beat down mercilessly on Sampaguita. Not a breath of wind ruffled the palm leaves. The dogs lay panting in the shade. The streets were deserted.

As he was passing the bank Juan was surprised to see the doors open and an important-looking man, dressed inappropriately for the weather in a suit, hurry down the steps. Hailing Juan he climbed into the *kalesa* and sat down heavily. "To the house of Principal Ramirez," he ordered.

Later, in the cool of the evening, Juan was chatting with the other *kalesa* drivers outside the Catholic Church as they waited for the *novina* to end. He mentioned his interesting passenger. "It must have been one o'clock. What would he be doing at the bank at that hour? Everyone goes home at noon."

"Ah," said Celso, always ready to pass on information. "I know the one you mean. My niece Luningning works at the bank. She says that they are being audited by the Central Bank. That man is the auditor. Principal Ramirez of the Elementary School is his wife's cousin so he is staying with him."

Two days later Juan met Celso at Juanita's *tuba* stall near the town *plaza*. Celso had been drinking and was already exceedingly eloquent, if repetitive.

"Juan, come here," he called as Juan passed by. "Have a drink. Juanita, give Juan a drink!"

Juan settled down beside Celso on the two bamboo poles that served as a seat and gratefully sipped the *tuba*.

"Have you heard the latest?" asked Celso breathing heavily in Juan's face.

"The latest about what?" enquired Juan, moving away a little.

"About the bank!" announced Celso with great importance.

Fixing Juan with his reddened eyes he declared, "You remember we were talking about the auditor at the bank? Well, Luningning says he's uncovered the most terrible scandal. Dr Lopez is as crooked as a corkscrew. She says he's fiddled the books and siphoned off hundreds of thousands of *pesos*. There's a typhoon of a row going on."

Juanita in her soiled Mother Hubbard dress leaned on the uneven counter and interjected, "Terrible gambler, that Dr Lopez! I always said I couldn't understand where he got all his money from. Always going off to Manila gambling, he is. He always bets big money too. You men are all the same. Terrible suffering it brings to your families!" she asserted, giving Juan a meaningful glance.

During the next few days the town was agog with the news of the bank scandal. It was almost the only topic of conversation. The embezzled sum was so vast that the local peasants could hardly conceive of such an amount and spoke about it in awed tones.

Dr Lopez had been absent for several days facing a Board of Enquiry at the Central Bank of the Philippines. Local rumours spread rapidly. Wild speculation about the punishment to be meted out to him even included life imprisonment and death on the electric chair.

Suddenly, to the amazement of all, it was announced that the chairman of the Central Bank had intervened in the enquiry and dismissed all the charges against Dr Lopez. He was only to be removed from his present position as bank manager in Sampaguita and given an inferior post in the distant island of Mindanao.

In Sampaguita this dramatic news sparked off long discussions and speculation by the townspeople on the cause of this reprieve. Was it political intrigue or bribery? Who could have interceded so effectively for him?

A surly and bitter Dr Lopez arrived back in Sampaguita the

next day to settle his affairs and to move his family to Mindanao. Unwanted furniture and belongings were put up for sale. His henchmen moved swiftly to collect the debts still owed to him. Their own payment depended on it.

Juan was sitting drowsily in his *kalesa* waiting for passengers outside the town hall when one of Dr Lopez's henchmen climbed aboard, jerking Juan back to consciousness.

"To the home of Dr Lopez," he ordered.

Juan cracked his whip and in no time they reached the imposing residence.

"Pull into the yard at the back," he was commanded.

There an irate Dr Lopez met him, doing nothing to control his temper. "Juan," he bawled, "where is the money you owe me?"

Juan was completely taken aback. "I'm sorry, sir, but I haven't been able to earn it yet," he replied respectfully.

Dr Lopez became angrier. "Pay me immediately or you'll be in trouble." he yelled.

"But I can't, sir," pleaded Juan. "I'm doing all I can, but I earn so little and my family is large."

"All right," glowered Lopez. "So you're not going to pay. I shall keep your horse and *kalesa* instead. I'll sell them to cover your debt. Now get out of my sight! I don't want to see you again!"

Juan fell on his knees and pleaded, "If you take my *kalesa* I'll have no way of earning a living and my family will starve."

"What is that to me?" retorted the heartless Lopez. "You owe me money and you are going to pay! Now, go away!"

Juan could do nothing but stumble home and lie moaning on the floor of his shack, his bony calloused hand wiping away the tears he could not control. Bit by bit Rosa extracted the story from him. She was furious. Dropping the dress she had been patching she ran to Dading's house. Not even pausing to be invited up she breathlessly climbed the steps and rushed inside.

The surprised *barrio* captain was resting, for it was still very hot, but he roused himself. Sitting with what dignity he could in his shorts and vest he listened sympathetically while Rosa panted out her news.

Dading frowned and his kindly face creased understandingly as he pondered the problem; then abruptly standing up he said, "Go home now, Rosa. Juan needs you. I'll see what I can do."

By evening the news of what had happened to Juan was all over Santo Domingo. Approving and even affectionate looks followed the upright figure of Dading and several of his village councillors as they left to call on Dr Lopez in Sampaguita. But their efforts were unavailing. The bank manager was adamant. Juan owed him money and Juan must pay. He also made it clear that he would scarcely change his mind to please a mere *barrio* captain, Captain Mahjong turned *Protestante* at that. As he was leaving in a few days' time he did not mind whom he offended. He would permit no one to interfere with his private business affairs.

Mayor Abando's intercessions later that evening also proved ineffective. Dr Lopez was in no mood to yield to pressure. The whole of Santo Domingo and Sampaguita was stirred to anger by the arbitrary seizure of Juan's horse and *kalesa* by a disgraced scoundrel. Urged on by the popular outcry Mayor Abando saw one slender possibility of helping Juan, however, and welcomed the opportunity to enhance his standing in his constituency, for municipal elections were drawing near again.

Early the following morning Juan in his best, neatly darned clothes was seated beside the mayor's chauffeur, with Dading and the mayor in the back seat, heading up the Manila road. Two hours later they pulled up outside the great Central Bank in the capital. Would Pedro Marcos, Chairman of the Central Bank of the Philippines, be willing to use his influence on Dr Lopez, the man he had just befriended in the face of serious charges?

Eventually the small delegation was ushered into an impressive office. Chairman Marcos listened patiently while Mayor Abando presented the problem and, questioning them carefully, became increasingly agitated. Anger showed in his voice and expression. Thumping his desk he exclaimed, "He shall not escape trouble this time!"

Pressing a button on his desk he summoned his private secretary. "Take down a telegram to Dr Lopez of Sampaguita," he ordered.

The interview was soon over but the result no one had foreseen. While the Mayor and his companions were driving back from Manila, Dr Lopez in Sampaguita was reading and re-reading a telegram with increasing anguish.

"THE UNFORGIVING SHALL NOT BE FORGIVEN STOP CENTRAL BANK INVESTIGATION INTO ALLEGED IRREGULARITIES TO CONTINUE STOP REPORT TO THIS OFFICE IMMEDIATELY STOP CRIMINAL CHARGES BEING PREPARED. PEDRO MARCOS. CHAIRMAN CENTRAL BANK OF THE PHILIPPINES."

In the car Mayor Abando and Dading discussed the situation.

"I can't understand anyone being so heartless as Lopez," remarked the mayor. "He was forgiven his huge debt, yet he could not forgive Juan's small one."

Dading nodded. "Very strange," he said. "You wouldn't believe it could happen."

"According to the payments Juan has made," continued the mayor, "he repaid his loan long ago. The high rate of interest Lopez set was illegal. It was intended to keep Juan permanently in debt—a victim of extortion. I suspect that a good many more people here are in the same position. We will look into it. They will be glad to see the back of Lopez."

"Yet in a way," said Dading thoughtfully, "we can do just the same as Dr Lopez."

"What do you mean?" asked the mayor turning his head sharply. Juan in the front seat pricked up his ears too.

"Well, I was thinking—God is good to us. He has forgiven

us our sins and yet we fail to forgive people who offend us, often quite trivially. Why, we harbour grudges and bad feelings for years."

Mayor Abando smiled. "Just like you to think of something like that, Captain. I hear you are doing some preaching nowadays. We'll have to call you 'Pastor Mahjong' for a change." He chuckled. "When do you preach next at the chapel in Sampaguita? I'll risk committing a mortal sin to come and hear you. Father Areta can be pacified! And by the way, let me know if any more of your church meetings are disturbed by bricks being thrown on the church roof. I have an idea who's doing it. He's too full of *tuba* most of the time to see what a transformation has come over some of you 'Bible Christians'. Is that what you call yourselves? Quite a useful name, in a country where just about everyone considers himself a Christian."

"Kind of you!" said Dading, and thought, "But we'll stick to reporting to Higher Authority."

8 SMOKING FOR PROFIT

Pedring lay sprawled in the shade of an enormous mango tree. His brother Berting sat hunched up, leaning drowsily against its trunk with his straw hat jerked forwards over his eyes.

It was hot. The paddy fields beyond them shimmered in the mid-day heat. It seemed to the brothers that the sweltering heat of the sun was specially focused on Santo Domingo. There was not a sign of life. Even the sparrows were panting with open beaks in whatever shade they could find.

"There's not a breath of air today," moaned Pedring, fanning himself gently with his straw hat—gently, but the exertion made him hotter.

He shook off a few persistent flies, attracted to the scratches on his arm made by the sharp thorns of the bamboo thicket where they had been felling several long, mature bamboos. But a moment later the flies returned. He wrapped his handkerchief around his arm but still the flies came back to torment him.

"Why did God make flies?" he asked, irritably swatting at them again.

Berting moved to a more comfortable position. "Dr Lopez has been recalled to Manila. What's going to happen to him now?" he mused, harping on the latest major topic of conversation of the whole area.

"He won't get away with it this time. You can be sure of that," Pedring murmured, his eyes still shut. "The old fool has only himself to blame. Deserves all the trouble he has brought on his own head."

"But old Juan hasn't got his *kalesa* back yet," yawned Berting. "He's really on his beam-ends now."

Pedring fanned himself again with his hat. "Last night I heard Dad inviting him and Ricky to help harvest our rice when it's ready," he said in the same monotone. "That should help them a little."

"But can he keep going for another couple of weeks?" Berting wondered. "I hope he gets his horse and *kalesa* back before then."

A long silence descended and Berting almost dozed off. .

Pedring still lay on his back thinking. His sleep-glazed eyes saw only a blurred image of the spreading canopy above him. A bead of perspiration trickled from his forehead and disappeared in the black hair of his temple. An unseen lizard rustled the dry leaves nearby.

"I wonder how old this tree is?" he asked almost inaudibly as he gazed up at the mango tree's huge boughs.

Berting only grunted.

"It must be very old," Pedring went on in the same expressionless voice. "Just look at those branches. It must have been a full grown tree when the Philippines was still a Spanish colony."

Pedring paused and continued staring up at the thick dome of leaves high above him. "There is nothing like a mango tree for cool shade on a day like this," he added, brushing off several ants that had decided to investigate him.

"I could do with a good ripe mango right now," murmured Berting, suddenly coming to life.

"I'd rather have an unripe one with some salt," yawned Pedring. "Who'd think it was the mango season. I can't see a single mango on this tree."

"No," said Berting with emphasis. "There's nothing on

earth so good as a good ripe mango," and as his eyes searched
the tree overhead, "not one to be seen!" he agreed. "It's
years since this tree produced any fruit."

"Well," said Pedring. "We haven't smoked it or slashed it,
have we?"

"No, I don't suppose we have," agreed Berting, uncom-
fortably remembering why—his own long absence from
the farm. "But even so you'd expect some fruit, wouldn't
you?"

"Not unless you prevent the flowers dropping and the
insects getting at them before the fruit sets," Pedring said.

Berting stood up and stretched his cramped legs. "Come
on, Pedring!" he said, rousing his brother. "We can't stay
here all day. I'll bring the *carabao* from the wallow and load
the sled. Time we dragged the bamboos back home. Dad'll be
up from his *siesta*."

Pedring's only reply was a long yawn. Then sitting up he
brushed a host of scurrying ants off his trousers and T-shirt
and clambered to his feet.

Hours later they were still hard at work. Berting bobbed
down to avoid the beam over the narrow doorway as he
carried in another sack of rice on his shoulder.

"It hasn't taken you long to bring another load," called his
father with approval as he paused in his hammering.

"No time to lose today," replied Berting resting the woven
palm leaf sack on another while he quickly untied the vine
holding the sack's mouth. "I've never seen such a harvest in
all my life. Don't know where we are going to put it all!"

Dading heard him grunt as he lifted the sack almost six feet
to pour its contents into an enormous round bin made of
woven bamboo. "Wonderful!" he said. "How the Lord has
blessed us this year. No drought and no plague of rats. We've
a lot to be thankful for."

Patiently the *carabao* waited while the remaining four sacks
of rice were unloaded from the sled and poured into the bin.

Berting wiped the sweat from his face and arms and walked over to where Dading was working.

"My! What a difference you're making!" he said. "We won't recognize the place when you have finished."

Dading stood back to survey his work. "It's certainly a good idea to have houses on stilts. If you've got the bamboos it takes no time to enclose the underneath part and make a store-room."

Berting nodded. "I never imagined that we'd ever need so much space to store our rice," he said.

"I'm afraid I'll need a couple more big bamboos to finish this job," Dading called out as Berting threw his empty rice sacks on to the sled and set off for the fields again.

Dading's eyes followed the strong, energetic form of his son. He marvelled at the change in him since he had come home a prodigal. "He scarcely seems the same man," Dading said to himself. "Indeed he isn't; Jesus has transformed him!" Removing his battered sweat-stained straw hat and closing his eyes, Dading thanked God for what He had done. And then he sighed, "Do the same for Pedring," he added.

The house was bulging with rice, downstairs and up. A good proportion of it had already been sold to old Mr Tan, the Chinese merchant at the "Sampaguita Trading". The Aranas family still dealt almost exclusively with him, never forgetting how he had saved Leon's life during the Japanese occupation. Yet even so the huge bin under the house was full and in the house itself every room had its quota of sacks until the floors sagged under the weight.

But now the time had come to collect the coconuts again. One of the great advantages of coconut palms is that once they start to bear, after eight to twelve years' growth, they go on doing so unceasingly. The coconuts are harvested every forty to sixty days. Pedring and Berting were going through their coconut plantation with a sharp curved sickle at the end of a very long bamboo pole, cutting down the ripe nuts. It required considerable skill to balance the pole and cut down only the heavy, ripe coconuts so that when they crashed to the ground they fell clear of the harvesters. Cases of tragedy were not unknown in the Santo Domingo area.

Pedring was cutting and Berting gathering, while Dading drove the *carabao*-sled to and from the copra-drying fire near the road. After all the harvesting had been done there was the back-breaking work of splitting the thick husk off each coconut, breaking the nuts in half and baking them till the flesh separated from the shell as copra. It had been a long hard day, and it was not surprising that Pedring's attention wandered from his dangerous job.

"Berting!" he called. "We could do with a drink of coconut milk, couldn't we? Shall I bring down an unripe nut or two for you and Dad while I'm about it? I could put away a gallon myself."

As he spoke he tugged at his bamboo and for a moment carelessly looked across at Berting, stacking coconuts for the next sled load. A massive green coconut, sure source of a long cool drink, came crashing down. It glanced on his upheld pole, diverting its fall, and before he could jump aside the coconut caught Pedring on the side of his head and felled him to the earth.

The clatter of the falling bamboo reached Berting and he shouted in alarm. Where Pedring had been standing a moment before, he was not to be seen. No, there he was, motionless on the ground!

"Dad! Dad!" Berting shouted. "Bring the sled. Pedring's hurt!" and raced to Pedring's side.

Dading heard the words "sled" and "Pedring". The tone of Berting's voice told him something was badly wrong. But Dading had not served as an infantry sergeant during the war for nothing. Nor was he *barrio* captain because he made good speeches. In fact his words were few, though each one counted. With a pounding heart he stood stock still for a moment, collecting his thoughts. Then, "Lord, we need Your help. Lord, save Pedring!" and he jettisoned the load of coconuts, turned the *carabao* and urged it into an ungainly

canter through the plantation towards where his sons were
working.

Berting was kneeling beside Pedring, mopping his own
brow with one hand and fanning him with his straw hat in the
other. Dading gasped when he saw the deathly pallor of
Pedring's face. He squatted beside him and felt his pulse,
racking his brain for memories of what first aid was needed.

"Stop fanning," he said. "He's in shock, cold and clammy.
He needs to be kept warm."

Though he said it, in his heart he feared that Pedring was
already dead, his cold sweat simply not evaporated yet. He
pulled open Pedring's shirt and put his ear to his heart. The
sound of a distant, faint heart-beat lifted the dead-weight of
fear.

"Thank God!" Berting heard him whisper. "Turn the
sled," he told Berting, "and help me lift him on."

Together they took Pedring to the copra-drying fire and,
leaving him on the sled beside it, unhitched the *carabao* and
tethered it where it could graze. Slowly the heat restored the
colour to Pedring's face while Dading and Berting waited.

"Lord, do not take my eldest son before he has yielded to
You," Dading prayed in his heart. "Give him another chance.
Remember the parable Jesus told. Don't cut him off like a
barren tree!"

To his surprise Dading felt what remained of anxiety and
strain melt away from him. His heart was at peace again.
Surely God was saying, "He'll be all right."

Dading looked at Berting, standing motionless beside his
brother. His lips were moving. He was praying too. As
suddenly, he stopped, looked surprised and turned towards
his father, questioningly.

"Yes," Dading said, interpreting his look. "I think God has
told us He is going to give Pedring another chance."

A long sigh came from the sled—from Pedring's body. Any
onlooker would have said it sounded like the death sigh. But
Pedring opened his eyes and closed them again. "My head,"

he groaned. Then Dading noticed the swelling beneath his thick mop of hair, becoming matted with blood.

Darkness was falling and the bats were wheeling overhead. The crimson sky had gone unnoticed. So accustomed to brilliant sunsets were they all in that part of the Philippines, that they would scarcely have given it a thought in any case, but tonight they could think of nothing but Pedring's deliverance. The evening breeze had died down and in the distant *carabao* wallows the bull frogs were croaking in an orchestra of syncopated sound. Had the paddy fields been full of water, instead of dry and parched—waiting for the irrigation system to be flooded again and the next crop of miracle rice to come in—the noise would have been far greater.

Pedring was lying motionless on the sled, wearing the dazed scowl of a man with an almighty headache, but able to talk. Shame that an experienced farmer like himself should have met with such an accident was his first reaction. In the tight little *barrio* community of Santo Domingo it would never be forgotten. For years he would be the butt of his *tuba* stall companions' wit. But he knew, as well, that every wisecrack would have the undertone of congratulation on his escape from death or disablement.

"Did you collect the sickle?" he asked.

"Yes. You've had a long sleep," Berting answered.

"We're ready to set fire to the grass and go home," Dading added. "Do you feel fit to move?"

Berting thrust an old dried palm frond into the glowing embers of the copra fire and had an ideal long-lasting torch for firing the heaps of tinder they had made at intervals between the towering palms. Soon the whole plantation was filled with the eerie yet attractive light of the spreading fires. The long coarse cogon grass, much of it yellow and dry, crackled and burned like a prairie fire, sending the hidden rats, mice and snakes scurrying and slithering in a desperate race to reach safety. It would not be long before the blackened, burnt earth would be covered again with fresh green shoots of grass, making a better pasture for the *carabaos*.

It was not long before the flames died down and could be left to burn themselves out. Gently Dading guided the sled along the rutted farm track, past the great mango tree, to their home. Pedring settled down on his sleeping mat, wanting nothing but to be left alone, and Berting stayed with him. In the silence Berting realized to his surprise how disappointed he was not to have gone with Dading to old Mr Madrid's new home in Sampaguita, for the Fellowship Hour.

Since his conversion Berting had been genuine in joining the Christians. Pedring no longer sniped at him for what he judged at first to be sheer hypocrisy in exchange for a home and livelihood. Instead he saw that Berting was losing his indolence, his craftiness and his foul language. Now, there was something interestingly like Dading about him instead; quite a change. But Pedring also saw that meetings after a long day's work in the fields had become more attractive since Chaling Madrid came home from college, proud possessor of a teaching diploma in Home Economics. Industrious by nature and fond of her now elderly parents, she had accepted a post in the Sampaguita high school and set up a little dress-making business on the side, in an annexe to their home. Whenever there were no evening activities of the church, her treadle sewing machine hummed busily, turning out Spanish-style "Maria Clara" dresses with butterfly sleeves, as well as the popular Mother Hubbard for a growing clientele of customers.

Pedring recovered quickly. To show that it was "nothing at all"—not worth a *tuba* stall guffaw—he went back to the plantation within a week and finished the job they had been doing.

One evening as Pedring shovelled the last fragments of copra into a sack Dading expressed his concern.

"I'm afraid our copra yield has dropped during the last couple of years," he said.

"That's what the irrigation channels have done for us," Pedring replied. "So much water is good for the rice but bad for the palm trees."

His father agreed. "I've noticed the palms at the lower end of the plantation, near the new paddy fields, have very few coconuts now," he said. "Their leaves are yellow and unhealthy."

"Some have almost ceased to bear," Pedring went on. "I think it would be better to cut them down and to extend the paddy field."

"You're right," replied Dading. "One or two certainly ought to come down. There is also the old mango tree. It's years since it bore any fruit. It is only occupying good ground to no profit. That ought to be felled too. We have more than enough to do without trying to coax new life out of that."

"Oh, Dad," interjected Berting, turning up at that moment, "that tree used to bear the best mangoes in the district. I can remember people coming to buy the most delicious great mangoes you ever saw."

"I remember you falling out of it and almost breaking your neck," chuckled Pedring, "But we never told Dad or Mother. Remember?"

Berting chuckled too. "I'll never forget that!" he replied. "I thought I would never be able to stand up again. Can't imagine how I didn't break any bones."

"If I had known I would have chopped it down immediately," Dading growled.

"That's why we didn't tell you!" his sons replied together, laughing.

"With the new irrigation channel," Dading continued, "it would be easy to turn that land into a paddy field. Just think how much miracle rice we could reap from the huge area covered by the limbs of that great tree."

"But if it bore fruit like it used to we could earn hundreds of *pesos* from it," argued Berting. "Let's leave the mango tree, and fell the dying coconut palms."

"Give it another chance," urged Pedring. "I'll undertake to slash and smoke it. We'll see if it will bear again. I'm sure it will."

"Mangoes are strange trees," Dading admitted. "You may be right. Well, if you're prepared to have a try, we will leave it for another year. Then if it doesn't come up to your hopes we'll fell it."

Pedring was as good as his word. During the following February he rarely missed a day, for several weeks, when he didn't have a smudge fire sending up thick clouds of smoke into the tree. And he slashed its trunk with his *bolo* to retard the excessive surge of sap.

He was not to be disappointed. A mass of blossom appeared and by the end of April the great boughs were bending under the weight of ripening fruit.

"A good crop, isn't it?" remarked Pedring to his father with obvious pleasure.

"More than I ever expected," Dading said approvingly. "You have been well repaid for your efforts." Then he fell silent, clearly in deep thought.

"What's up, Dad?" enquired Pedring.

"Oh, sorry," Dading replied. "I was thinking of your accident."

"Why that, of all things?"

"It suddenly struck me that we've seen a living parable."

"A what? I don't understand."

"I'll tell you," Dading answered. "It was when you were unconscious and I thought you would die. I prayed that God would spare you—like you and Berting pleading to give this tree another chance. I felt then, immediately, that God had heard and answered Yes."

"Another chance?" said Pedring casually. But he turned and slowly walked away, trying to appear unmoved.

9 OUT FOR A DUCK

The bus was speeding southward from Manila, on its way to Sampaguita.

"Do you mind having the window shut?" asked Captain Mahjong. The gusty night breeze was not only cool but showered the passengers with dust blown up from the bus floor.

Lito was sitting by the window. He fumbled for a moment with the piece of hardboard that served as a shutter and then had it up and rattling loudly in its frame. Several other passengers had already pulled up their shutters and those on the completely open side of the bus had pulled down the rolled plastic rain curtains to the floor. At last the gale tearing through the bus was under control.

"Pity these shutters don't fit like the ones you made for your house on the hill, Lito," commented Dading, shivering and pulling his hat down more tightly on his head.

Lito smiled. Jim Evans folded his arms more tightly to try to keep warm. "I could do with a sweater over this thin shirt tonight," he said.

"I thought you 'Americanos' never felt cold in our country," said Dading with surprise.

"I must have Filipino blood by now after all the rice I've eaten," Jim answered, shouting to be heard above the din of rattling and of the inadequately muffled engine. "So I feel just like you do."

They were returning from committee meetings of their Fellowship of Churches. It united churches in Manila and several provinces. Dading and Lito were delegates from the little congregation in Santo Domingo.

As the bus slowed down on the outskirts of a town, several teenagers suddenly jumped aboard on both sides of the moving bus. There was room for their feet on the open luggage racks running the length of the bus, below floor level, and a hand-grip on the window frames. They let down the shutters from outside with a bang, simultaneously bawling out a non-stop, raucous repetition of the wares they carried in baskets over the crook of their arms. "*Mais! Mais!* Maize!" one girl with streaming hair and faded dress shouted through the window beside Lito.

Jim pulled his purse from his pocket and bought six steaming hot corn-cobs. The bus braked suddenly as it stopped at the bus station. There was only a moment for the transaction. The driver and conductor were hurrying home. Quickly the girl wrapped the corncobs in a strip of banana leaf and took the coins.

A young fellow with sharp, bright eyes and a fog-horn voice climbed into the front seat and turning to face the passengers reeled off like a machine gun, "*Balut! Penoy! Balut! Penoy!* Oy, mister! *Balut—balut—balut—balut!*"

Dading signalled to him. In a flash he disappeared and almost instantaneously reappeared beside Dading.

"Three!" ordered Dading. "I want *balut*, not *penoy*," he insisted. *Penoy* are ordinary ducks' eggs hard boiled.

"These are *balut*, sir," replied the boy. "See, they have a cross on them," and he pointed to a pencil mark on the eggs. "They're not a day less than two weeks old."

The bus started and quickly accelerated. The boy shouted, "Just a moment! Just a moment! Someone's buying something!" but the driver took no notice.

Quickly taking his payment the boy handed over three *balut* and three tiny packets of salt. Then holding with one hand to the side of the bus he jumped with a well-practised movement.

For a moment they could hear the hard patter of his feet in the darkness and the bus continued to gather speed.

"Nothing like a *balut* when you are travelling!" Dading said enthusiastically. "Let's eat them while they're hot."

He tapped the broad end of the duck's egg on the wooden seat in front of him and peeled off part of the shell. Inside, it was like no ordinary egg. Only a thin soup was to be seen. Opening his packet of salt he sprinkled some in, then raising the egg to his lips he noisily sipped the juice. Jim did the same.

"A bit like crab—with a touch of Marmite!" he thought.

Dading peeled off more of his shell and sprinkling a little more salt into it, bit off some of the solid part of his *balut* as if it were apple. He was obviously enjoying it immensely.

Jim wished the fourteen-day-old duckling didn't look so revolting. Closing his eyes he decided not to look more than necessary. The feathers, or veins or whatever the black part was, were slimy and tasteless. Then there was the yellow part and a white, rubbery, chewy part, and distinct suggestions of duck meat and tiny bones.

By the time he had finished eating he wondered why Westerners made such a fuss about *balut*. It was "not bad at all". And how satisfying it was!

"Delicious!" he replied with permissible exaggeration when Lito simply raised his eyebrows to ask how he liked it.

"You are a real Filipino if you eat *balut*," declared Lito. "You can understand why there are so many duck farms. Sometimes the ducks are taken many miles to find new feeding grounds."

A few weeks later Dading was feeding his black sow under a large acacia tree near their house. He poured the swill into an enormous white clam shell which served as a pig trough and stayed on guard until his pig had finished guzzling. Its squeals of delight at Dading's approach had alerted a couple of the neighbours' free range pigs.

Shameless poachers, they were only tolerated because they kept the neighbourhood free of refuse, eating anything edible they could find. But their presence meant that someone must stand guard while the Aranas's own pig was being fed.

While his sow was busy, Dading washed her down with a bucket of water and his hand. As he finished a jeepney stopped on the road outside his house. He stood up to see who had arrived but didn't recognize either the jeepney nor the young man who climbed out and approached him.

"Good morning, sir," the stranger greeted him politely.

Dading nodded.

"Is this the house of Captain Aranas?" enquired the man.

"Yes, I am Captain Aranas," he replied with a perceptible straightening of his back and squaring of his shoulders. "What can I do for you?"

"I am Rolando Ilagan, sir, I have come from Manila."

Dading cleared his throat.

"I have brought a load of ducks," Rolando continued. "If someone would give me permission, I would like to let them glean where the rice has been harvested."

Dading thought before replying. "This is a long way for you to come," he said. "But I have no objection and I don't think the other farmers will mind—so long as you don't get up to any tricks."

"Oh, I'm not like that, sir," smiled Rolando.

"You'd better start in my paddy fields then," said Dading, pointing the way. "You can ask the other farmers for permission later."

"Thank you very much, sir," Rolando answered with relief, turning to unload his ducks.

"And, by the way," Dading called after him, remembering his responsibility as *barrio* captain to provide hospitality for strangers, "You'll need a place to stay over night. You can sleep here with us: and cook for yourself if you like. We'll find a spare rice pot for you."

Dading watched while Rolando and the jeepney driver unloaded several large plaited bamboo crates full of loudly protesting ducks and showed him where he could leave his old guitar and plastic shoulder bag in the house.

Then Rolando took his carrying pole, slipped each end through the ropes of a crate, placed his shoulder under the pole and a moment later was jogging at a steady trot towards the paddy fields with the crates swinging rythmically fore and aft.

When all the crates had been carried to the feeding ground he released his ducks. They greeted their freedom with noisy appreciation and a great flapping of wings.

Accustomed to being herded, they quickly adjusted to their new environment and Rolando settled down under the shade of a tree to keep an eye on them, lest any should stray too far.

When Pedring and Berting arrived home at sundown they found that Rolando had already corralled his ducks for the night and was sitting on the steps of their home in the soft evening light playing his guitar with unusual skill.

"Ha! Serenading tonight!" declared Pedring enthusiastically. "I'll rally up the boys. OK, Rolando?"

"Whatever you say," Rolando agreed.

After their meal Pedring and Rolando changed into clean shirts and combed their full black hair as glamorously as any woman, dowsing it with highly scented pomade.

"Aren't you coming?" asked Rolando, seeing Berting making no move to join them.

"He's given up serenading!" laughed Pedring. "Since he became a *Protestante* he doesn't live it up with the rest of us. Anyway his girl is in Sampaguita—a member of their church. She wouldn't approve of him serenading!" There was mocking in his voice.

Berting chuckled. "Thanks for the invitation," he said to Rolando. "We're having a special meeting for the harvesters tomorrow night here in this house and I've got to get ready. An *Americano* missionary is coming. I hope you'll join us. I think you'd enjoy listening to him. There'll be music too. New tunes for you to pick up."

"It wouldn't do me much good," replied Rolando, still combing his hair at the mirror. "I don't understand English."

"Oh, Jim Evans talks our language like a Filipino," explained Berting.

Satisfied that he was looking his best, Rolando turned and picked up his guitar. "That's a different matter, then," he replied belatedly, intense concentration before the mirror ended. "An *Americano* talking our language could be entertaining. OK, I'll join you tomorrow night."

As Pedring and Rolando wandered along the unlit street to collect the rest of the young men, Pedring said, "Serenading has come to have a bad name in this area. Some fellows have behaved badly. They've drunk too much and been irresponsible. The girls' families won't stand for it."

"Not only here," agreed Rolando. "When the girl being serenaded won't come and sit with a light at the window, some guys stone the house."

"Just so," Pedring said. "They can't really object, either, if the parents oppose serenading while their daughters are working for exams. The girls haven't the time to sit at the window for hours, just to please a few young flames. Recently the trouble has been that while some are singing at the front of the house, others are stealing the chickens at the back. In Sampaguita we have to get police permission to go serenading, so that they know who is responsible. Here in the *barrio* we don't need to bother. Anyway, my dad won't put up with any misbehaviour."

When about a dozen of his friends had joined them, Pedring led the way to the home of a girl in whom he was interested.

The doors and windows were closed up for the night when they arrived, but a light in the living room shone through chinks in the palm leaf walls and window shutters and through the split-bamboo floor, dimly illuminating the area beneath where a pig and a couple of goats were tethered to the stilts. A dog near the steps barked angrily.

Pedring's friends stood around or squatted wherever they could, chatting together until Rolando tuned up his guitar and started playing. Then Pedring began to sing, with Rolando accompanying. A few romantic songs and then the crucial one which invited his young lady to take her place at the window.

From the first notes of the serenade the family in the house had been anticipating this moment and the young men outside could imagine the whispers and gesturing that were taking place inside.

The window shutter creaked and Edna propped it open with a bamboo pole. She pulled a chair up to the window, put an oil lamp on the window sill and sat crocheting where her admirers could see her. Late into the night she and her family and the neighbours on their sleeping mats were entertained by Rolando's superb guitar playing and Pedring's haunting Filipino love songs.

Dading grunted his disapproval at being roused from deep sleep in the early hours by the noisy return of the two serenaders. But when dawn broke it was his turn to awaken Pedring for another day's harvesting.

Rolando shuffled off to attend to his protesting ducks and guided them through the muddy rice paddies using a long bamboo pole with a tuft of leaves at the end. Slowly but greedily they gleaned their way to a distant field where Rolando had noted the old mango tree.

"Just the place for my midday rest," he said to himself.

By noon his loss of sleep caught up on him. The sun was beating down fiercely but in the deep shade of the tree it was pleasantly cooler. The ducks were close at hand and resting contentedly. He lay down and almost immediately fell asleep. Hours passed. The deep shadows began to lengthen and creep out over the field.

He awoke with a start and, not having a watch, he checked the position of the sun, low in the sky. Instantly he jumped to his feet. His ducks had scattered far and wide. Picking up his bamboo switch Rolando set off to round them up. Running along the narrow banks between the paddies and splashing slowly through the muddy fields he herded the flock together and drove them as quickly as possible towards their corral near Dading's house.

As they were crossing the last paddy field he suddenly remembered that he had not counted them. When they were all spread out feeding in a field they were not difficult to count, but herded together it was impossible.

For a moment he wondered whether he should try to count them or leave them unchecked till the morning. But his conscience was troubling him. He stopped and encouraged the ducks to disperse in the field. Then he started to count them. On the first count one duck was missing but he felt no alarm. After re-counting several times, however, and reaching the same conclusion he realized that he would have to act quickly or be in trouble with his employer.

Without delay he drove the ducks into their corral. As he closed the rickety wire-netting door he saw that the light was fading and a bat was already swooping round the jackfruit tree.

Rolando ran to the house. "Berting!" he called. Berting was feeding the black sow. "Can you lend me a torch? I've lost a duck and it'll soon be dark. I don't want to lose my way in the fields."

Berting hurried into the house.

"Don't be too long, Rol," Berting said as he handed him the torch. "Remember our meeting tonight. You promised to come. You mustn't miss hearing the *Americano*!"

"As quick as I can," Rolando shouted back as he ran towards the paddy fields.

With his bamboo in one hand and the torch in the other, he ran as far as he could along the narrow banks between the paddy fields, retracing his steps and looking everywhere for the missing duck. Several times he stumbled and almost toppled into the muddy fields.

The big red sun was sinking all too rapidly below the horizon and he urged himself forward even faster. "In a few minutes it will be dark," he thought. "What a fool I was not to count them immediately. Now I'll never find it."

While crossing a palm-log bridge, he slipped and fell sprawling in the mud, and as he fell he dropped the torch. Precious time was lost while he groped around in the slush till he found it. Dripping wet and plastered with mud, he tried washing himself in the irrigation channel. But then he realized water had got into the torch and it refused to work.

After the few minutes of tropical twilight it had suddenly become dark. But he had at least reached the place where the ducks had been foraging. And his eyes began to become adapted to the starlight.

Using his bamboo to investigate any bumps that showed up blacker than the rest, he still hoped to find the missing bird.

Suddenly he heard a noise like the crying of a puppy. He began to feel afraid. A snake somewhere nearby was swallowing a frog.

"What if I tread on a snake?" he thought. He prodded the path before him with his stick and stamped his feet to scare any snakes away.

The cry of a night bird startled him as it flew unseen across the fields. Rolando trembled. "Was that an *aswang*?" he wondered. His imagination conjured up the dog-like spirit, reputed to feast on the livers of the dead! The nearness of the spirit world made his flesh creep. He felt utterly alone and defenceless. "What if I am attacked by a *tikbalang* or some other demon of the night?" He tried to banish such thoughts from his mind and, crossing himself reverently, repeated several "Hail Marys" for protection.

"It's useless looking for that duck," he decided weakly. "I'll come out in the morning at first light. It will probably stay nearby—unless a boa-constrictor gets it."

He was on the point of turning back when something

moved. Momentarily he discerned the outline of a duck's head silhouetted against a silvery, starlit pool.

Gently he made his way towards it through the muddy field, talking to reassure the duck lest it try to escape, but it waddled away, anxiously quacking. Rolando pursued it but no matter what tactics he employed it always managed to keep a few yards ahead of him.

At last he managed to creep near, crouched, and then lunging forward caught the startled duck by one leg. It struggled frantically, neck elongated, wings flapping, but Rolando brought it under control and, clutched firmly under his arm, it soon settled down.

"Thank goodness for that!" he exclaimed. "Now for home!"

But he had lost his bearings in the darkness. Though he tried walking first in one direction and then another, he could discover no familiar landmark. His fears returned. His sense of loneliness intensified. He groped his way along the narrow banks, stumbling and slipping in what he hoped was the right direction. Thoughts of evil spirits and poisonous snakes continued to torment him—until the massive form of the old mango tree became discernible and he was on the right path.

Rolando dropped his delinquent duck safely in the corral and made his way over to the house. He was surprised to see it crowded with people and a group of men standing on the veranda. They were singing a song he had never heard before. The tune was a good one and from what he could pick out of the words, they kept repeating, "There's no Friend like Jesus, no one, no one," He stood hidden in the deep shadows listening.

After a while Rolando could hear someone descending the creaking stairs to the ground. It was Berting. He stood at the foot of the steps peering into the darkness and shone a torch around as if looking for something. Slipping his bare feet into his rubber sandals that had been left on the bottom step, Berting turned and was walking down the side of the house when he caught sight of Rolando.

"Ah, Rol!" he exclaimed. "There you are! I was coming to look for you; I thought you must have got lost. Did you find it?"

Rolando could not see Berting's face in the darkness but he knew from the tone of his voice that he was smiling, and wondered what made him so light-hearted all the time.

"It took a long time and I got lost finding my way back," Rolando replied, "But at least the duck is in with the others."

"Good!" said Berting, "I'm glad," and he went back to the veranda and called up quietly, "He's here. He found it!"

Two other young men joined Berting. "Glad you found it," they said. "Come and join us upstairs. It's a good meeting tonight."

"'Fraid I can't," explained Rolando. "Look at me! I fell in the paddy field."

They turned the torch on him and laughed. But he was still wet and shivering. Berting crept into the house by the kitchen stairs and found a change of clothing for him. Then the four of them rolled a huge rice mortar carved out of an old tree trunk under an open window where they could hear everything going on in the room above, and sat on it together.

Jim Evans was explaining a parable from the Bible and speaking about people being lost.

"Jesus is like that shepherd," he said. "He seeks for them till He finds them because He wants to rescue them from great danger and bring them to His home. Men are blind to the danger they are in, but Jesus came to make a way of escape. Devil and men did their best to defeat Him but He got the better of them all. He gave His life for us but He rose again. Nothing can stop Him now. Why keep running away from Him?"

Rolando nudged Berting. "Like my duck!" he whispered with a chuckle. "Could I catch it! But I did."

Something stirred inside Rolando. He had always thought

of Jesus as dead, gaunt and hanging on a cross or as a wax figure in a glass case in the church. "Alive and looking for me?" Rolando wanted to know more about this. "I'll ask Berting to explain when I've cooked my supper," he resolved.

And when everyone had gone home and Berting and his father were answering Rolando's questions, Dading noticed that Pedring was lying awake listening, in spite of his loss of sleep the previous night.

10 AGAINST THE GRAIN

Jim and Betty Evans had been visiting a little cluster of houses
out among the fields some distance from Santo Domingo. As
they carefully balanced their way along the top of a narrow
bank between the flooded paddy fields, heading for Dading's
house, they saw Pedring half way up his calves in the mud,
following a small Japanese tractor. Their *carabao* was still part
of the family, but this new investment was saving hours of
time spent on ploughing. In fact, one man with the tractor
could get through the same amount of work as ten men with
ten buffaloes. The wide, steel paddle wheels of the tractor
prevented it from sinking into the mud, and with its vertical
exhaust pipe stuttering noisily into the sky, it chugged busily
to and fro as fast as Pedring could lift his feet out of the sludge
and squelch them down again.

They waved him a greeting and he waved back cheerily.

"He's friendly enough," Jim said, turning to Betty. "Why
won't he take the Gospel more seriously?"

As they trudged and slithered along the path, Jim in
plimsolls and Betty barefoot by preference, they noticed at
stages along the bank and at the corner of each paddy field
some dried-out daubs of mud with little heaps of rice on
them.

"What on earth is this for?" said Betty poking at the rice
with her toes. "It has obviously been placed here very
carefully."

"Yes," agreed Jim. "It looks like some animistic rite to ensure a good harvest. But it can't be—this is Dading's land. He wouldn't make an offering to the spirits or be involved in any superstition now that he's a Christian!"

"Very odd!" said Betty doubtfully.

"Probably poisoned," Jim said.

"*Tao po!*" they called at the foot of Dading's veranda stairs. "There's someone here!"

Dading appeared in the doorway, as cheerful as ever, and invited them up. Dropping the plimsolls at the bottom they climbed up and sat on a bench looking out across the rice fields while Dading relaxed in his favourite rocking chair.

"How's old Grandpa Pabling today?" he asked. "Still standing up to his old lady?"

"Yes, we had a good visit," said Jim. "Both the families in that coconut grove have welcomed us since the meetings here last harvest time. We were able to leave a gospel and some other leaflets with them today."

"That's good," commented Dading. "I'm sure they will read it."

"They want us to visit them every week," Jim went on. "But it's almost impossible to find time for another home Bible study with all the other activities we have."

"They could come here," Dading said. "It isn't very far for them to walk."

"You know how it is," agreed Jim. "They give evasive answers—afraid of being called *Protestantes* if they attend our meetings, but glad to have us visit them."

"Those families are on Attorney Teodoro Marquez's land and he is a fanatical Catholic," Dading exclaimed. "They have to tread carefully. He might well eject them if he heard what they were doing."

"That's the man who filched Juanita's land soon after we came here, isn't it," Betty asked. "I thought he was too rich to care about what anybody believes. Hasn't his son become a leading politician and another been to the States?"

"Yes, the engineer," Dading said. "But the old man watches his interests like a hawk. You can't avoid persecution in this area if you become a real Christian." Dading thought deeply for a moment, then, "Look at Florencio in Sampaguita," he went on with feeling. "He was one of the first to be converted there. He was a terrible drunkard and gambler. He neglected his children and often beat his wife; in fact he had two wives. Then he was saved and his life changed. He let Number Two go, cared for his family, dropped his vices and worked hard at his carpentry. You know what happened. His relations were so mad at him for going to study the Bible that they made life miserable for him. Even his wife opposed him!"

"Incredible," sighed Betty.

"Just look at him now!" Dading went on. "He's just about back to where he started. But they all seem to prefer it."

"We've noticed," Jim joined in, "that among the more influential families becoming a *Protestante* is considered one of the worst of crimes.

"Yes, especially in these conservative country areas," agreed Dading. "'If we are going to go to hell,' they say, 'we'll all go together!'"

Dading suddenly jumped up. "I'd forgotten I'd put the coffee on. You'll have a cup with me, won't you?"

They went through into the simple kitchen.

The dark wooden walls were decorated only by two large calendars. One was from the nearby Shell garage and the other, in Chinese, English and Filipino, from Mr Tan's "Sampaguita Trading". They sat down on benches round the plain board table.

Dading poured the steaming hot coffee into thick white china cups and opened a can of sweetened condensed milk.

"On the way here," Jim said, "we noticed little heaps of rice on the banks between the rice fields. What are they for?"

"Oh," answered Dading with concern on his face. "I hope you didn't touch it. That rice is poisoned—the most deadly poison I know. We put it out to kill the rats. If you had touched it with your hands you would need to wash very carefully lest you poison yourselves. We wouldn't like to lose you just yet," he laughed. "This year the rats are destroying a lot of our seed rice. But they are very cunning, they seem to know when it is poisoned."

"We noticed that all the dogs in this area are tied up and all the hens are in enclosures," Jim said. "We guessed it might be something like this."

"The rats come out of their holes at night," Dading continued. "Pedring and Berting have been going out with flaming bamboo torches lately, hunting them. With good heavy sticks they are able to kill any number. The rats can't move fast enough in the mud. Some evenings it doesn't take them long to fill a couple of five gallon kerosene cans!"

"This way. Follow me!" called Dading. "You can't leave without having a word with Berting. He's in charge of transplanting the seedlings."

"You are always planting or harvesting rice," laughed Betty.

"Yes," agreed Dading. "Since the government put in the irrigation channels from the river we have been able to grow rice in the dry as well as the rainy season. It has meant a lot more hard work, of course."

They reached the lush green seed beds where several workers were tying up rice seedlings in bundles. Standing barefoot in the mud they worked at an incredible speed, pulling out the seedlings and whipping strips of cogon grass round them, all in one movement. Others were with Berting, planting the seedlings in twos and threes in a nearby paddy field. They worked in a long row, moving backwards as they planted.

"My word!" exclaimed Betty. "I don't think I have ever seen hands move so quickly before. How do they do it?"

"Just practice," said Dading smiling. "But it is backbreaking work. Do you know the song about it?" And he started to sing:

> 'Planting rice is never fun;
>   Bent from morn till set of sun;
>   Cannot stand and cannot sit,
>   Cannot rest for a little bit.

> 'Oh, my back is like to break;
>   All my bones with bending ache;
>   And my legs are numbed and set
>   From their long soaking in the wet.'

"Cheers!" exclaimed Betty. "We'll be forming a choir in Santo Domingo yet!"

Berting reached the end of his stretch of field and came over to join them.

"Thanks for bringing them, Dad," he said. "Say, Jim and Betty, will you come to my wedding when the planting's finished? It's all been arranged and Pastor Ilaw is coming to conduct it. . . ."

Berting was marrying Chaling Madrid, the bright young school teacher. His father, as custom demanded, had visited Chaling's parents in Sampaguita some time previously and arranged the date and details with them. In the Filipino tradition the expenses of a wedding are the responsibility of the groom and his family, so Berting and Dading had been doing some careful budgeting.

Berting bought for Chaling a beautiful white wedding dress, which also according to tradition, she was not permitted to try on until the day of the wedding. Scissors, needles and thread had to be ready for rapid alterations if the dress didn't fit! Fortunately, Chaling's fitted perfectly when the day came. For himself Berting bought a magnificently embroidered, white *barong tagalog* shirt. So much had happened since he, the family ne'er-do-well, had come home penniless. Now he was a member of the New Creation church in Santo Domingo, and so transformed that no one for a moment thought of his seamy past—except Pedring, puzzled and envious of his brother's happiness.

Both the Madrid and Aranas families were large and respected, so Dading expected a host of visitors, relations and friends. They decided to have the wedding at Sampaguita where the half-completed chapel was at least big enough.

The church members undertook to do the decorating, but when the day came they had done much more, they carried the building project almost to completion. With the artistic ingenuity of their race they then transformed the interior, all to show their affection for Chaling, Berting and their parents. Banana palms had been cut down and the green outer layer of the trunk removed to produce the perfect imitation of glistening white marble pillars. Potted plants and flowers festooned the chapel. People passing on the street stopped to admire the display.

Before the service the pews were linked together all down the aisle with chains of fragrant sampaguita buds, the national flower. The place was crowded. Marcing, the town photographer, was everywhere with his bulbs flashing. Several present had never before set foot inside a *Protestante* church and had qualms about being there—until to their relief, they saw the Madrids' neighbour, Mrs Gonzales, the leading Catholic lady of the town, looking as unrepentant as she was resplendent for the occasion.

Ramon Ilaw was at his best. He never let an opportunity like this be wasted, but today he had the right thing to say for everyone. It was all happiness for the bride and groom and encouragement for the church members. He explained so meaningfully, step by step, that no one failed to understand what was going on.

"The Church is the bride of Christ. He makes us His own spouse if we want Him," said Mrs Gonzales to her husband that night. "No one ever told me that before, but there it is in black and white in your Catholic Bible, just like theirs. Beautiful, I call it."

The feast was held in the garden at Chaling's home. A special awning had been erected over a long, improvised table seating fifty people at a time, with bride and groom at opposite ends. Plates of rice and pickles were on the table and pork, chicken, goat and beef dishes cooked in a variety of ways, and slices of a pig roasted whole, were served at intervals by a succession of waiters. There seemed to be no end to the courses. Then last of all came a sweet dish, followed by the customary glass of water.

Later that evening when most of the guests had left, Berting joyfully drove his bride to his family's home in Santo Domingo, in their newly-acquired jeepney, an investment capable of providing a livelihood during off-seasons on the farm.

The next day was Sunday and in Sampaguita Father Areta was preaching an unusually stern sermon.

"Some of our members," he thundered, "seem to have forgotten that it is a mortal sin to enter a church of another religion. It is with intense sorrow that I inform you that some of our members, including one of the most devout, committed this offence only yesterday. . . ."

The worshippers left the mass whispering to one another, "What does he mean? Who was it?" Word soon got around—no less a person than Mrs Gonzales was on the receiving end of the *padre*'s rebuke.

Nor was the message lost on the redoubtable Mrs Gonzales. That noon Father Areta waited patiently in his *convento* for his lunch. He was enjoying his book, but feeling a little hungry he glanced at his watch. "Ah, my lunch is late," he muttered to himself. "It is usually here by now." He adjusted his spectacles and settled down for a few more minutes. But there was no sound of footsteps coming to his door. He heard a *kalesa* approaching and looked expectantly out of the window, only to see Juan pass by.

At last he drew the right conclusion, stood up, threw his

book down in great annoyance and with simmering anger lit his kitchen stove, washed some rice and put it on to boil. For years his Sunday lunch had been sent round from Mrs Gonzales' lavish table. How intensely he regretted that his sermon had destroyed a tradition so very dear to him. But he was no weakling. As he ate his rice and sardines he pondered how to right the situation. What was salt in his wound, however, was that by nightfall the whole parish would be enjoying the joke.

It was most unusual for Jim to find Captain Mahjong discouraged. This time he was really depressed.

"What's the problem?" asked Jim. "The drought?"

"Yes," Dading sighed. "This is the worst drought anyone in this area can recall. The water in the river is down to a trickle. Come with me."

Together they walked out to the rice fields. The sun blazed out of a cloudless sky as it had for many weeks. Even the cogon grass was brown and withered.

"There!" exclaimed Dading pointing to one of his paddy fields. "Look at that! That rice had just got going nicely when the water level in the irrigation channel fell too low to reach this far. The ground has set like concrete with cracks so wide and deep you can put your hand in them. Even some palm trees have died and their tops have fallen off," and he pointed to a nearby knoll. The headless palms looked like great posts pointing to the sky.

"To think that only last year you had to enclose the area under your house to hold all you reaped," Jim said. "Can you trust the Lord now, as you did then?"

Dading gave him a look, thought a moment and said, "Thank God, I can. Before I knew Him I relied on my own devices. Have you heard? There have been some ugly scenes over the water supply. The irrigation officials worked out a rota to give all the farmers a fair share, but during the night some farmers have shamelessly dammed the channels and diverted water on to their own land. When it is our turn we have to be out all night to make sure no one is doing that to us. We sometimes have to clear a blockage or we wouldn't receive a single drop."

"It's hard for the farmers to watch their crops die off and not be able to do anything about it," Jim sympathized. "No wonder they grab all the water they can. But as *barrio* captain you're in for big trouble if that happens."

"Yes, already there have been some serious fights," replied Dading, "and I'm afraid that if this drought continues someone's going to get murdered."

"I hear there's a court case on now, against a farmer who beat up an irrigation supervisor when he refused to let him have more than his fair share of water," Jim said.

"Yes. It's the same old story. When bribery fails they resort to violence. They'll do anything when their livelihood's at stake. It's hard enough for us Christians to wait and see what God is going to do. Perhaps the Lord is teaching us not to take His blessings for granted."

They walked on in silence for several yards and then Dading asked "By the way, how are your Bible studies going with the families in the palm grove? I haven't heard anything from them for weeks."

"I came over today to talk with you about them," replied Jim. "We had quite a crowd for the first few meetings. Then, as usual, after the first flush of enthusiasm, most stayed away."

"The devil's rats got into your seed bed!" Dading interjected.

"That's about right," agreed Jim, "Unless it's the drought. Old Grandma Onching is our big problem. She is a real old battle-axe. Most of the people living there are related to her and the old matriarch rules them with an iron hand. When she is around the attendance drops dramatically."

"I'm not surprised," chuckled Dading. "I know her well!"

"Several of the younger people had shown quite a bit of

interest," continued Jim. "I thought one or two of them were actually believing, but after she went for them with her sarcastic tongue they kept away from the meetings. Now their interest seems to have withered and died, like your rice in the parched paddy fields."

Dading nodded. "I was afraid that would happen," he commented. "But how about Grandpa Pabling?"

"Oh, he's our main-stay in that community," answered Jim. "Although he is the husband of Grandma Onching, and looks an inoffensive, meek old man, he refuses to be intimidated. And there are two or three other men who stand with him. From what we see and hear they're 'new creations' already," and he gave Dading a wink.

"That's wonderful news," exclaimed Dading.

"They are talking about attending the Sunday morning services here in Santo Domingo," Jim went on, "so don't be surprised if they turn up. Their faith is maturing rapidly. At least the drought has given people time to think about more important things."

"How about the rest?" Dading enquired.

"I think Tomas and his family would genuinely like to become Christians but they earn most of their living by raising fighting cocks and operating an illegal gaming pool. They know they would have to leave the gambling business and aren't prepared to face that cost."

"Gambling does develop an awful grip on you," Dading reflected. "I'm sorry I spent so much of my own life gambling, and I'm glad that Jesus helped me to break free from it. Anyway, let's see what happens at the harvest meetings," Dading said. "I'm praying that Pedring will take the plunge then too."

A lively bunch of harvesters were hungrily enjoying their evening meal together in Captain Mahjong's house. Several of Dading's relations had come to help with the harvest. They all enjoyed being together at these times. The drought had broken just in time to save most fields and the rats migrated elsewhere. A hard day's work had given everyone a good appetite. Plates were piled high with rice, and Chaling, the new daughter-in-law, had prepared a tasty dish of chicken spiced with a little onion, vinegar and soya sauce, which they all liked. A spiralling truss of bananas stood on the table and as each one finished his meal he broke off a banana, demolished it in no time and drank a glass of water.

Before they left the table Dading interrupted the flow of conversation by calling out, "By the way. Tonight we are going to start something special. We are having five nights of meetings here in this house and I hope you will all be able to stay and listen. I'm sure you will enjoy it."

"Will it be like the meetings last harvest time?" someone asked.

"Yes," Dading answered. "The *Americanos* are coming again and bringing Pastor Ilaw and a group of young people from Sampaguita."

"And the highlight," Berting butted in with mock pomposity, "is a duet by Chaling and me. Don't miss it!"

His words were drowned by rowdy applause and banter. Under cover of the disturbance Pedring slipped out through the kitchen. "Why do I always have to feel so uncomfortable on these occasions?" he thought.

Chaling was scraping out the rice cauldron. "Aren't you going to stay?" she said. "It won't be the same without you. It's fun being all together."

Pedring scowled. "I'm going down to the *tuba* stall as usual," he muttered. "I'll be a sight happier there."

Chaling looked crestfallen. "Sorry," she said.

"It's like living in a church in our house," retorted Pedring sullenly. He grabbed his straw hat, quickly ran down the stairs, crossed the yard and turned down the road towards the village. The sun was just setting, streaking the sky with crimson, against the darkening palm trees. A bonfire of burning rice straw glowed in the distance, but Pedring in his annoyance saw none of it.

The house that night was jammed with harvesters, mostly

young people from distant places where the Christians seldom managed to go. Even Rolando Ilagan, the duck farmer, had come from Manila. Old Grandpa Pabling had arrived in good time after a long walk across the rice fields. He sat in the rocking chair on the veranda happier than he had been for a long time. Others from the coconut grove arrived later and had to sit on the floor or stand in the doorway. Three hours passed like half an hour, everyone so enjoyed the singing and the illustrated talks given by Jim Evans and Pastor Ilaw. They were still there when Pedring came back from drinking with his friends. He was a moderate drinker, so the gloom had disappeared and he was feeling friendly when he propped himself against a doorpost and listened. It was Jim speaking. "Not a bad fellow," thought Pedring. "Interested in the farm. . . . Even gives a hand sometimes."

"Trouble is, we're all like this farmland," Jim was saying, and Pedring pricked up his ears. "If it isn't floods, it's drought. And if it isn't rats, it's locusts. All our backbreaking work, planting the good news about Jesus—He came for you, He died for you, He rose again for you, He's alive today for you, remember?—and something or other seems to shrivel it up or swallow it up. Look, friends, it's all for you! Open your hearts to God's message that He gave us to bring. Let the Holy Spirit of God irrigate it. Let His sun shine on it. Share the harvest of happiness and new life that you can't help seeing in some of your friends here who have done it already. . . ."

In spite of himself Pedring was hanging on every word. When everything was over and groups of people were setting off together into the brilliant moonlight, Pedring found himself one of several squatting in the yard with Rolando and his guitar. At first Rolando was trying to pick up some of the hymn and chorus tunes he had learned during the evening. Then he drifted into his serenading tunes.

"Come on," Pedring said after a while, "There's still an hour till midnight, and just look at that moon! Let's see if Edna feels like listening tonight."

Ramon Ilaw and Jim were still on the veranda with Dading. "The rats are at him again," he said.

But Edna was away at a relative's harvest supper. When Pedring and Rolando came back they sat out under the stars talking. And Dading heard one of them say, "You've got to admit it, this 'new creation' business seems to work."

11 DEAD OR ALIVE

The most important day of the year was dawning. In Sampaguita it was strangely quiet, not like a usual Friday with radios starting to blare, people bustling about their business even before the sun rose, and noisy tricycles with deafening Japanese motorcycle engines straining to pull their overloaded sidecars.

This was the Friday of Holy Week. All through Lent the excitement had been building up, though the chief indication of it was the mournful singing of a dirge known as "The Passion", a lament about the sufferings of Jesus. Many of the conservative rural familes believed that it was specially meritorious to have the "Passion" sung in their homes at least once during Lent and particularly during Holy Week. Hired singers, suitably dressed in black, continued singing throughout the night, their stamina maintained by a free supply of beer and cigarettes.

On the previous Sunday, Palm Sunday, Father Areta had been busy sprinkling holy water over palm fronds brought to the church, and during the last few days young men known as *murions* had been patrolling the streets. They were dressed like the Roman soldiers who arrested Jesus, and their grotesque, gigantic masks featured everything from fierce Roman soldiers to comic, anachronistic figures with spectacles. Their helmets and hats were crowned with tufts, sprays and tassels in every colour. And their clothing, anything from imitation armour to a caricature of a toreador, with embroidered, flowing capes, presented a riot of colour in the drab streets. With sticks, swords and spears they scoured the town all day long "looking for Jesus", to the terror of the small children who scampered home shrieking at their approach.

On Easter Sunday morning they would chase round the town in pursuit of "Longinus", supposedly the centurion of the guard which crucified Jesus. According to legend, after the resurrection of Jesus these soldiers realized their mistake in putting to death the Son of God and, seizing their officer Longinus, beheaded him. To the amusement of Sampaguita's townsfolk their local Longinus would eventually be arrested, brought to the town *plaza* and ceremoniously "executed". Neither they nor the crowds who watched their antics had any concept of what the Resurrection meant. They would understand that a seed must die in the process of bringing new life, but the death of Jesus was little more to them than another religious legend, like the *murions*, and His resurrection merely a theological dogma.

Jim and Betty woke early this Holy Friday morning, disturbed as much by the unusual quiet as by the sound of neighbours chopping wood, blowing up their fires and opening their shuttered windows. There was a lot to do. The Santo Domingo Christians were coming to spend the day with the Sampaguita congregation, and the missionaries were to make them welcome. Therefore the bare wooden floors must be polished till they shone like the sun, reflecting the glaring light outside.

As the morning progressed Jim and Betty heard a strange, wailing chant approaching down the street. Going to the window they saw a man dragging an enormous cross. He wore a wreath of leaves on his head and several palm fronds tied to his waist trailed behind him like a ragged train. A pathetic little group of older women dressed in black shawls and dresses followed a few yards behind him. In the centre of the group one woman held a tattered copy of the "Passion" which they were wailing unmusically.

"Look," muttered Jim through the side of his mouth, "It's Floring, Pedro's wife—defender of the faith, queen of all superstitions. And Lito thinks his pal Pedro is all but believing already. It'll take a miracle to get her converted."

"Did you see her self-conscious glance in our direction?" Betty whispered. "We're to blame for making her man kick over the traces. But I thought she seemed quite friendly last time we met her on the beach, didn't you?"

"Perhaps she's understanding the gospel better," Jim said. "Let's hope this is her final fling."

The sound of a slow, rhythmic click-clacking drew their attention. Looking away down the street they could see a similar group of women dressed in deep mourning and also singing the "Passion". This time, however, a man, stripped to the waist, was scourging himself as he strode mechanically in front of the singers.

"Oh, isn't that terrible!" exclaimed Betty. "He is beating himself with every step he takes! It must be very painful. Just listen to the crash of that scourge on his back!"

She wanted to see no more and went back to the kitchen. Jim stayed at the window.

Slowly the sad procession passed, to the moist, thudding rhythm of the scourge. Jim stared at the two large raw patches on either side of the man's back, inflicted by the beating. Children playing in the street stopped, mesmerized. Others ran to the security of their homes and from the steps watched in wide-eyed terror.

At the end of the rope scourge splayed out about twenty five-inch bamboo sticks, red with blood. Jim racked his memory. The penitent looked strangely familiar, but the wreath of leaves and veil of rags half covering his face prevented recognition.

"I've got it," he said to himself. "That's Rosa among the mourners. It must be Juan. Poor Juan! Always in trouble. If it isn't fighting cocks and gambling it's too much *tuba* and brawling. He's got plenty to be sorry for. But this! How can I show them that it gets him nowhere?"

Farther along the street a little shrine had been erected by the roadside: a framework of bamboos hung with delicate lace covers over a couple of candles and an image of the Virgin Mary. Juan had just reached it. Jim saw him kneel and then lie prostrate with his arms stretched out in the shape of a cross. His scourge, wet and sticky with blood, lay beside him picking up the dirt. His followers chanted their dirges. Then he rose and went on, flailing himself mechanically, not sparing himself at all.

"When he gets home he'll bathe in the sea," thought Jim. "It seems to keep their wounds from going septic." And then, "Hello, Betty, you back again? D'you know, that was Juan, the *kalesa* driver. It'll be days before he's fit to work again. He's a genius for keeping his family at starvation level, isn't he. People say the *flagellantes'* wounds heal quickly because they were gained in doing penance but you should have seen how raw he looked."

"At least the RC Church is embarrassed by all this sort of thing," Betty answered. "And some of the priests oppose it. I heard that a German priest threatened to shoot any *flagellante* who tried to enter his church! But his parishioners told him he was only objecting because he hadn't the courage to be a *flagellante* himself!"

"It's a hang-over from the Spanish colonial days, of course," Jim said, "and customs introduced two hundred and fifty years ago take a long time to die out!"

A jeepney packed tightly with people drew up at the door.

"Cheers! It's the Santo Domingo folk," and Jim made for the stairs and clattered down to the front door with Betty following more cautiously.

Berting was climbing out of the driving seat and Dading and one of his young nephews from the passenger seat on the other side, but the back of the jeepney was disgorging a seemingly endless crowd of people, Lito and his wife Myrna, Rene and Lydia, Berting's cousins, Chaling and, to Betty's delight, Edna, who only last year had been carnival queen in the *Flores de Mayo* celebrations. This was something new, a brave thing for her to do. She would be taunted for associating with the *Protestantes*, especially on Holy Friday of all days.

"Come in. Sit down and rest!" Betty said as she ushered them all in. "It's hot already today. I know you'd like a drink of water. Give me a hand, Chaling, will you?"

She led the way to the refrigerator and they filled up two trays of glasses, each with a jug of water with ice cubes.

"Pedring's coming too," Chaling said under her breath.

"Pedring!" Betty repeated.

"Yes, partly because of Edna and partly to see the *flagellantes*. But I think there's more to it than that."

Dading and Jim were sitting in the living room with the others.

"The rest are coming as soon as they can find a jeepney," Dading said. "There are very few running today and so many people are heading for Sampaguita. We left in good time to make sure of some time with you before the service started." They sipped their iced water.

"Aren't you one of the speakers today, Dading?" Jim asked.

"Yes." He smiled. "And so is Berting."

"The first time you've spoken in the church here in Sampaguita?" Jim said, turning to Berting. "I'm glad you've been taken on to the team of preachers."

"I feel more nervous than when I gave my graduation speech," Berting replied.

The little chapel in Sampaguita was packed with Christians from the surrounding *barrios*, and still more had to stand outside by the windows and in the doorway to follow the service. A number of people who had shown some interest at

Home Bible Studies but who never normally attended church services were also in the congregation. Pedring turned up at the last moment and had to wedge himself in beside a doorpost. That Berting was to be one of the speakers intrigued him immensely. What exactly had happened to this prodigal brother of his? But it was a bit worrying that Chaling and Edna were becoming good friends. He hadn't reckoned on Edna becoming a believer.

"We need a bigger chapel already!" Pastor Ilaw remarked to Jim.

Ramon Ilaw had recently moved to Sampaguita as the first pastor of the growing church.

"It's the right sort of problem to have. I wish we ran out of seating at every meeting," replied Jim.

The service took the traditional form of a Filipino Good Friday service with seven speakers giving short addresses on the "*Pitong Wika*", the "Seven Sayings" of Jesus on the cross, interspersed with hymns, and readings from the Gospels. Dading was the sixth. "It is finished".

"What was finished?" he asked. "A full and complete satisfaction of every requirement for our justification before God. Jesus died so that we can live. His work was final, once for all. But His death was also a beginning. It is the death of the seed that liberates new life and makes the harvest possible. 'Finished' for Him means 'begun' for us. . . ."

The service lasted nearly three hours, but afterwards the Christians were loath to separate and go home. They stayed chatting and enjoying each other's company, and later settled down to discuss the problems created by the approaching town *fiesta*. Those who had only recently become Christians were trying to work out how time-honoured Filipino customs were affected by their new faith. So many of the accepted practices were either Roman Catholic or superstitions or else simply worldly in nature.

Mr Madrid, Chaling's father, put the issue clearly. "Our problem is," he said, "that the *fiesta* is held in honour of the patron saint and the focal point is the Mass in the Roman Catholic church. We could work out what is religious, what is superstition and what is harmless social custom in the events of the day, but few people distinguish like that between one event and another."

Buxom Mrs Cruz, the Sampaguita Restaurant proprietor's wife, joined in. "Trouble is," she said, "most people who come to the *fiesta* don't attend the mass and half the visitors from a distance scarcely know who the particular saint of this town is, so in actual practice the *fiesta* has little to do with the saint or the Mass in his honour."

"True," replied Mr Madrid, "but we shouldn't lose sight of the actual significance of it however many people regard it as only a social occasion. Devout Catholics still emphasize the historic and religious meaning of the *fiesta*. If we join in with them it will be assumed that we share their views."

Jim thought he heard a sigh go round the room.

Mrs Madrid supported her husband. "We feel," she said, "that we must completely dissociate ourselves from the *fiesta*. I'm not even going to do any special cooking."

"But what will you do when your visitors arrive?" someone asked. "You are sure to have friends and relations calling on you. What will you do if you have nothing to put before them?"

"We will just have ordinary food," replied Mrs Madrid. "Then if they are really coming to see us they won't mind, but if it's the *fiesta* and feasting they want . . ." she paused and with an "everything's settled" sort of smile concluded, "they won't come back next year!"

The others chuckled and wished the answer was as simple as all that.

"I would be embarrassed if I had nothing special for my friends if they called on me," admitted Lito's wife, Myrna. "It would look so rude, however good my motives."

"My husband isn't a Christian yet," joined in Mrs Cruz. "He would be mad with me if I didn't do everything as we have always done it."

"It's easy for those who are married and have Christian homes," said Lydia, still in her teens, "but my parents are not believers and I will have to work all day long at *fiesta* time, cooking for our visitors."

"That's right, Lydia," interjected Pastor Ilaw. "You must obey your parents in so far as it is possible for you, as a Christian. The Bible makes that very clear. And the same is true for you, Mrs Cruz, in your relationship with your husband."

"But what about contributions to the *fiesta*?" asked a prosperous-looking man in his late thirties. He owned a furniture and carpentry shop and was expected by the *fiesta* organizers to contribute generously towards their funds. "Any day now they will be going from house to house collecting money. It will be very difficult not to give the same amount as in previous years. What do you think we ought to do?"

"Yes," said Pastor Ilaw. "This is your first *fiesta* since you came to know Jesus, isn't it. It is going to be hard to be different. It is important that we should stand firm on whatever Christian principles are involved and ask God to give us tact and wisdom in the difficult situations in which we will find ourselves. This will be specially true for those of you who don't come from Christian homes. Persecution is hard to take, but remember Dading's Easter message. The seed must die. If it dies it becomes fruitful. Die to yourselves and live to God, and we shall see many more people turn to Him as a result. But what about contributions to the *fiesta* funds? How is this for an answer? We want to contribute toward the good activities and let our position be clear to everyone on the bad and doubtful ones. We want nothing to do with the cabaret or gambling, the cock-fights or fortune-telling, but we'll back the sports events and music contests generously, don't you think? Shall we offer a prize for the children's sports or the basket-ball tournament?"

The discussion went backwards and forwards, with Pastor Ilaw and Jim and Betty drawing attention to scriptural principles to help the new believers reach the right conclusions for their own particular circumstances—to be positive rather than negative in their attitude to the *fiesta*.

"Let's try to use the *fiesta* day as effectively as possible for our Lord," they stressed. "If you have visitors in your house, talk openly with them about your Saviour. That will show that you are not just a *fiesta* fan like so many. Then there'll be our bookstall near the *plaza*. The site is already booked. Mr Madrid made the final arrangements yesterday. We've ordered a good stock of Christian literature, gospels and Bibles from OMF Publishers in Manila, and five thousand tracts for us to distribute. With people coming miles and miles from all around Sampaguita, this is our best opportunity of the year to contact them. Let's pray that another *barrio* church will result from our *fiesta* efforts this year, shall we?"

"And before I forget," Ramon Ilaw continued, "if any of you can stay behind for a while after the youth meeting next week you can help stamp the tracts with the name of our church so that interested people can contact us."

Eventually they had to wind up and those who had any distance to go made their way to the market-place. There the jeepneys and buses waited until they were packed to capacity, with more passengers having to cling on to the back and sides if they were to get home at all.

The sun was already sinking low in the sky when Dading and the Santo Domingo party finally dragged themselves away.

Somehow eighteen of them managed to climb aboard Berting's jeepney, and a dozen more packed Jim's smaller jeep. Dading was sitting by Jim and as they drove down the main street he said, "Do you know the superstition that is common among our people here? They say that 'God is dead' on Holy Friday and doesn't come to life again until Sunday of the Resurrection. So they think they can sin like the devil because there is no one up there to keep a record until Sunday morning."

"How strange," remarked Jim "—to think that God could die and rise again every year—and not find out what happened in His absence! What better example could you find of the Devil blinding the minds of the godless and making them believe a lie? But do you know that in our country some people can't understand why we preach to Roman Catholics!"

Turning the corner they found the road blocked by an enormous crowd of people.

"You'd better pull in to the side," Dading advised. "This is the big procession forming up."

They waited while hundreds of people were slowly marshalled into position. Then the signal was given and the procession began to move forward. First of all came the little girls, all in beautiful white dresses, then older children and youth groups followed by women's guilds and men's organizations, with everyone carrying lighted candles. Several older women wearing the habit of St Anthony patrolled the teenagers' section of the slowly moving procession, rebuking irreverent chatterers and urging them to repeat the "Hail Mary".

Next came a large glass-sided coffin, borne along on the shoulders of eight men. Inside it Jim could see a grotesque, life-sized waxen image of Jesus, pale and blood-stained.

"See what I mean," said Dading to Jim. "This is how they think of Him. Stone dead."

"This kind of Catholicism seems to think of nothing else—except to worship Mary," remarked Jim.

"Yes, that's right," agreed Dading. "Before I understood the Gospel everything centred on the Mass. I never thought of Jesus apart from a crucifix. Although I knew vaguely that He rose from the dead it certainly didn't register with me that He really is alive right now."

Lito was apparently having the same thoughts. As the coffin

drew closer he started singing softly, "*Buhay! Buhay! Si Kristo'y
nabubuhay* . . ." At once the others joined in. It was one of
their favourite choruses. "He lives! He lives! Christ Jesus lives
today. . . ."

The coffin bearers stared at them as they passed, but
showed no sign of understanding. They had the same blank
expression, the moroseness, of almost everyone in the crowd.

Now the focal point of the procession was approaching, an
illuminated float. Trundled along on a cart drawn by a team
of strong men and lit with a score of electric light bulbs, came
an ornate image of the Virgin Mary dressed in deep mourning
and riding high on an elevated throne. Before it walked the
senior citizens and officials of the town, escorting old Father
Areta in all the grandeur of his finest robes. The mayor was
there, and Judge Sarmiento, Principal Ramirez and of course
Attorney Teodoro Marquez. Holding an open prayer book
but seldom looking at it, Father Areta was reciting over and
over again in a loud voice, "*Aba ginoong Maria, napupuno ka ng
gracia* . . . Hail Mary, full of grace!"

Among those near to Father Areta several were repeating
the prayer after him. Further away most of the marchers were
silent. Only a few said an occasional "Hail Mary".

As the float progressed along the uneven, potholed road,
the image of the Virgin wobbled dangerously, but there were
attendants to steady it. Behind came a jeep carrying a noisy
generator supplying the electricity for the lights around the
image, and two men were busy managing the cable between
the jeep and the float.

Sometimes the Virgin's crown reached perilously close to
the sagging telephone and power lines that crossed the street.
Two other men with long bamboo poles had the duty of
lifting them clear but it was more easily said than done. More
than once the image teetered near the point of disaster and the
gaps in the procession became wider and wider while the
hazards were overcome.

Following the generator came the *murions* and a few men

straining under the heavy crosses they had also borne earlier in the day. Then, finally two long, well-spaced lines of *flagellantes* scourging themselves.

With the road clear at last, Jim switched on the engine, slipped into gear and headed again for Santo Domingo. He was silent and distressed by what he had witnessed, but all the way home his Christian friends lifted up their voices and sang and sang, in celebration of the deliverance they had personally experienced.

Jim dropped his passengers at Dading's house and turned the jeep. Reaching Sampaguita again he found the road still blocked. It seemed that every man, woman and child who could walk was in the procession.

"Now what?" he muttered to himself. "Stop here and wait or trail along behind?" Then he noticed two men a little way off the road. He stopped the jeep near them and jumped out.

One, middle-aged and tough, was a *flagellante*. He was stripped to the waist with blood all over his back. The other was lacerating the *flagellante*'s back with a razor, carefully making two rows of incisions in a herringbone pattern.

The *flagellante* shook the ash off his cigarette and said, "Make a neat job of it! I want the scars to look good."

"They'll look good all right!" growled the man with the blade in a sepulchral voice.

Jim stood back a little. The stench of human blood and sweat was revolting. Then he said, "Do you mind me asking? Why are you doing this?"

"I'm being like Jesus!" the *flagellante* answered proudly. "There are fifty-two of us this year."

"Finished," said the man with the razor blade.

The *flagellante* threw the butt of his cigarette into the ditch, ran to catch up with the procession and fell into line flailing his scourge.

Jim had a bold idea. He slowly drove between the two rows of *flagellantes*, wondering what sort of reaction this would get, and was relieved to note only looks of surprise and approval. Some of the men even grinned at him.

Many of the *flagellantes* were beating their backs with each step they took; others, for whom the beating was now too painful, only continued scourging themselves when passing groups of onlookers. Some men were beating the front of their thighs as well as their backs.

Jim called out to one man, "May I ask what are you doing that for?"

"I'm being like Jesus!" he replied. And other *flagellantes* gave the same answer. It seemed to be the stock answer, as though this was the most natural thing in the world for anyone who wished to be like Jesus.

They were strong rough men.

"How much of this is sheer bravado, just to display their toughness?" Jim asked himself. "And how much is inspired by a desire to please God? What ignorance, if that's their motive!"

Some of the *flagellantes* were smoking and most seemed to have been drinking heavily. One suddenly broke ranks, jumped into the jeep and sat beside Jim in the front seat, regardless of the mess his blood was making.

Soon another man climbed up to join them. It was Celso from Santo Domingo.

"Why are you doing this?" Jim asked.

"My wife was very ill last year and I vowed to do this if the Mother of God would heal her," the first one answered.

"And you?" Jim pressed Celso.

He hesitated and then said in a rush, "If a guy is bad all through he's got to do something about it."

"But don't you know that Jesus went through it all for you?" Jim exclaimed. "There's no need to do it all over again. He was wounded for our sins and by His scourging we are healed, is what God's Word, the Bible, says. Come back to my house with me and I'll show you for yourself."

"I'll come when I've bathed my back in the sea," Celso said.

When Jim arrived home he found a few of the Christians
still chatting with Betty at the gateway.

"Hang on a while," he urged them. "I'm hoping one of the
flagellantes will come here soon."

Sure enough, a subdued Celso in a clean shirt and trousers
turned up an hour later. Together they talked and the
Sampaguita Christians explained in a way Jim could never do
in a language not his own, how Jesus took the place of every
sinner when He died on the Cross. Celso was spellbound.
"They never told me that", was all he could say.

It was late when Jim got out the jeep again and took Celso
home.

"I'll talk with Captain Mahjong in the morning," Celso
said as he waved goodbye. But on the way back Jim knocked
up Dading and told him what had happened.

"Praise the Lord!" he exclaimed. "I'll visit him tomorrow
if he doesn't show up."

12   FROZEN ASSETS

Old Attorney Teodoro Marquez slid open the windows of his bedroom and looked out. The windows, made of scores of square, semi-translucent clam shells set in wooden frames, let in sufficient light to inform him that the dawn had broken.

It had rained during the night and heavy drops fell from the nearby fruit trees whenever their leaves were rustled by the occasional slight breeze. The rain running off the galvanized iron roof of the old Spanish-style house produced a long, narrow puddle all along the side of the house under the eaves.

Attorney Marquez breathed in deeply, enjoying the fresh, cool, morning air. The sun raised itself up from behind a low cloud on the horizon and he felt the sudden gentle warmth of its first sharp rays.

"What a perfect morning!" he exclaimed to himself, and resting his hands on the window sill he breathed in deeply again.

The exceptionally long drought which had so disastrously withered the crops during the previous months had broken three weeks ago. The whole countryside was almost green again. Nature's surging new life was rapidly transforming the shrivelled, parched, brown landscape with new leaves and fresh, green shoots.

Attorney Marquez was taking another deep breath when suddenly, involuntarily, he stopped. Holding his breath he stood motionless and alert. For a brief moment he caught the sound of a band playing in the distance and with it his expression changed instantly to one of unutterable sadness.

Of course, it was *fiesta* day in Sampaguita. A flood of memories swept him right back to last year's *fiesta* when his son Bernabe had worked so hard as chairman of the organizing committee. But now he was . . . dead.

He abruptly left the window and, dressed only in his vest and striped pyjama trousers, wandered into the kitchen where his housekeeper was busily preparing his breakfast. He switched on the radio and almost immediately switched it off again, and slumped dejectedly into a chair at the table.

In the town the mood was in total contrast to the old man's melancholy. Gaily coloured bunting, most of it advertising rum, beer and cigarettes, was strung across the streets, creating a carefree atmosphere of festivity.

The specially hired brass band had started its tour of the town as early as six o'clock that morning, playing rousing music to the delight of the children who rushed to the gateways and windows of their homes to watch the smartly uniformed bandsmen pass down the street. Somehow the band could maintain the beat of the music without marching in step, and one or two members even found time for a quick puff at a cigarette while their comrades blared away all the more vigorously to make up for their silence.

At dawn the large bells in the high church tower had summoned the faithful and since then Father Areta and additional visiting clergy had been extremely busy conducting Masses. The church had been thronged for each service with gracefully veiled women and immaculately dressed men, for today was the feast of San Pedro (Saint Peter) the patron saint of Sampaguita.

Already a great many visitors had come to stay with friends and relations for the celebrations. Hundreds more would be arriving soon. Today every bus and jeepney in the area would be jammed to capacity with passengers clinging to the sides and backs of the vehicles as they made their way to the *fiesta*.

The mayor and municipal council had carefully considered their contribution to the festivities. They knew that one way to ensure their future re-election was to make the town *fiesta* a notable success. At all costs it must go off happily. For several days an army of the town's unemployed had been filling in the innumerable potholes in the streets with gravel, grass sods and soil, while others cut the grass on the neglected verges and in the "park". Additional lighting had been installed in the *plaza* where the *fiesta* ball was to be held, preceded by a firework display and the procession of the beauty queen. The "queen" was the young lady who had raised the most money for the *fiesta*. Her beauty was politely assumed. To be the queen or one of her "princesses" was to have a good place in the local marriage stakes. The princesses were other young ladies less successful as fund raisers. In the procession they would all be most lavishly dressed in magnificent gowns and, with their escorts in evening dress, would parade before the town accompanied by the band.

A theatrical group and a comedian from Manila were to perform on an open-air stage in front of the town hall. There would be sports for the children and a basket-ball tournament for the young men. A fun fair set up for a week with a full range of interests from a ferris wheel and shooting booths to gambling tables, a fortune teller, a nightly "floor show" and a display of nature's freaks, including a stuffed *carabao* with two heads and five legs. There was even a "live mermaid".

Along both sides of the main thoroughfare of the town and in part of the *plaza* were rows of stalls selling an incredible range of goods: clothes, belts and plastic bags, attractive shoes and slippers, flick-knives and daggers, besides china, enamel ware and a great variety of food. Among them this year was a novelty—the bookstall and display of Christian posters by the Sampaguita church. People strolling up and down to see the sights and spend their savings had to bob their heads frequently to avoid the low guy ropes from the awnings over the stalls, criss-crossing in every direction.

Many who were already deeply in debt had borrowed more money or extended their credit to entertain their *fiesta* guests and have a splash. To do any less would involve unthinkable loss of face. The blood-curdling squeals of pigs having their throats slit in preparation almost drove Betty to hysterics. Even when silence returned at long last she said, "I can still hear those pigs! They are worse than the deafening loud-speakers at the funfair."

Old Attorney Marquez sitting gloomily at his kitchen table could not isolate himself from the *fiesta*, but while his housekeeper fussed busily around him the old man sat lost in his thoughts about Bernabe, the last of his sons, now dead like the other two.

"Why, he was so popular. He revelled in this kind of occasion. He made a bad marriage, but he might at least have left me an heir—if he hadn't died. For a man of forty Bernabe was still pretty fresh—gave the impression of being several years younger. True, he had a reputation for being a 'play-boy' and a bit too fond of the bottle, but I'd never have called him an alcoholic. You couldn't blame Bernabe for slipping away to Manila whenever he could for a few days' night-clubbing with his wife. After all, Sampaguita's a dead and alive sort of place and a man's got to live."

The sound of the band came clearly through the window. They had started doing the round of the streets. The old man's thoughts came back to last year's *fiesta*. He could visualize everything so vividly. There was Bernabe on the stage receiving the acclaim of the appreciative crowd "for making the *fiesta* such a success". Little did he, or anyone else, imagine that within six months this fine handsome man would be dead. Bernabe had fallen ill and died in a Manila hospital on Christmas Eve. The result of alcoholism, they had said.

Attorney Teodoro Marquez was a remarkable man. His impact on Sampaguita had been enormous. Approaching Sampaguita from the sea one would hardly imagine that hidden behind the crowded fishermen's flimsy houses standing awkwardly on their stilts, and concealed behind the curtain of palm trees skirting the beach, lay a busy, thriving town. The fishermen's motor canoes pulled up in a line on the shore and one or two larger boats bobbing at anchor, used to ferry passengers and freight to neighbouring islands, gave little indication of the activity and importance of the town among the palms. A careful observer, however, could not fail to notice the two high buildings rising above the apparently endless sea of graceful palm fronds. They were the white bell tower of the Roman Catholic Church and the rusting galvanized iron roof of the Marquez Enterprises. Their prominence on the landscape was indicative of their importance in the town.

The Marquez Enterprises building housed, among other things, a massive rice warehouse, an ice plant, and the town's electricity generators. On still, warm evenings the monotonous throbbing of the diesel oil generators could be heard over a wide area and either effectively lulled the townspeople to sleep—or kept them restlessly awake.

There had been an electricity generator in the town some years before Teodoro Marquez took it over. In those days the generator had been too small for the ambitious, avaricious aims of its operator. Each house connected to the supply hopefully meant a bigger income for the proprietor. The antiquated machine had strained hard for four hours every evening to produce its maximum output to meet the demand. In the early evening when the load was greatest, the voltage had usually dropped so low that fluorescent lights could not be started without a booster and ordinary light bulbs produced little more than an apologetic glow. Moreover, the generator frequently broke down and the consequent delays for repairs, often prolonged while awaiting the arrival of spare parts from Manila, made the uncomplaining townspeople regard electricity as more of a luxury than a part of normal life.

Eventually the company had gone bankrupt and Attorney Marquez, astutely seeing the potential of this industry, acquired the franchise for Sampaguita and district. Immediately there had been dramatic changes. New, larger generators produced an adequate and steady current of electricity.

The town was most grateful for this improved service and when, a few months before the municipal elections the incumbent Mayor Abando had diplomatically installed a very simple form of street lighting, his friend Marquez had gained an additional income and the Mayor's chances of re-election had improved immeasurably.

The new bright lights of the town had their effect on the life of the community. People's habits changed. Instead of going to bed a couple of hours after sunset, they stayed up later and enjoyed more social life. The Abando–Marquez alliance became almost invincible.

Eventually the Marquez Enterprises provided electricity for twenty-four hours each day, unwittingly introducing a new range of status symbols. Electric irons and refrigerators, television, electric fans and floor polishers began to make their appearance in the wealthier homes. Also the quiet of the town was shattered for hours on end by the blare of record players and radios turned up to serve everyone within earshot.

The house lizards, the geckos, also approved of the better lighting which powerfully attracted insects at night and their colonies increased in number in every house. Never before had the people of Sampaguita seen such enormous clouds of insects as those that now sometimes danced and whirled around the new, bright street lights, luring swarms of flying termites to their death in the cavernous mouths of frogs and toads. Two cinemas vied fiercely with each other for popularity. Amost every day a jeep from one cinema or the other would slowly tour the town with gaudy posters and loudspeakers advertising the latest film.

Now, as he drooped at his breakfast table, the very picture of misery, Attorney Marquez was living his life over again.

"It hasn't been worth the effort," he groaned. "I would have been a Senator at the very least, after my successes in the bar examinations. 'Top-notcher' in my graduation year at the University of the Philippines, I would have made a success of politics if only I had been able to call upon some influential backing and money. Instead I had to resign myself to being a lawyer in a one-eyed provincial town. As if the country was not already overstocked with lawyers! Pah! Too many of them sink into being rural hacks. I did at least add a few strings to my bow, a few judicious business investments—and not a few little enterprises off the record!" The old man almost cheered up, recalling how within a few years he became one of the most wealthy men in the Sampaguita area. But with a sigh he sank back into his dismal reverie. His conscience was bitterly attacking him.

"It was a case of every man for himself after the War," he tried to argue. "After all, everyone's title deeds had been destroyed. It was a case of your memory against mine. How could I be sure of where my boundaries lay? They had to be re-established. It was done in the courts by due process of law. Why should people smear my name with accusations of land-grabbing?"

Visions of Juanita and numerous other victims of his schemes crowded back to accuse him, but he fought on. "I've been the greatest benefactor in this area. Who hasn't profited from my success and who has been a better son of the Church? How often have I missed Mass?—when I was free to attend it. Who has old Areta turned to when he needed help? 'Father' Areta! I've been a father to him, even if he has a year or two's lead on me! No one would think I'm as old as I am, or as sick. My hair's as black as anyone's, thanks to the

Chinese dye! Don't I pass for a mere sixty-year-old—except to those who've seen me around for so many years!"

Slowly his self-congratulation restored some of his confidence, and the strong sweet coffee gave him new vigour. He stood up and shuffled over the gleaming hardwood floor to the window again. Decades of polishing with coconut husks had given the beautiful floorboards a patina like glass and he always had to move carefully. The view from the window was so familiar that he normally gave it no thought. Today, however, his reminiscences brought it sharply into focus. Across the *plaza* and beyond the ancient buildings of the *convento* his massive warehouses, rice mill and generator plant reared their rusting hulks like temples of mammon, shamelessly rivalling the church. Away past the squatter area of the town, the chimneys of the Sugar Central stood, surrounded by his sugar cane fields, and up the slopes of the foothills acres of his citrus and coconut plantations shouted prosperity to all who saw them. Pride swelled in the old man's heart. "Work and wages for hundreds of my fellow-countrymen," he said to himself. Never having known anything of the sweated labour and dire poverty among his employees he was blind to the misery for which he was personally responsible. Had he seen Juanita setting up her *tuba* stall with five times as much highly-fermented coconut sap as usual, he would have turned away in disgust.

Attorney Marquez had always been a stern employer and decisive business man. Anyone delinquent in paying for his electricity immediately had his supply cut off. On the first day of each month he sent one of his decrepit old trucks around the town. In the back of the truck, suspended on a chain stretched tightly between the two sides, was a very large bell. As the truck lurched slowly along the potholed streets, the clapper gave out an irregular sequence of ear-splitting dings and dongs. Prominent in the back of the truck was a large black notice board bearing in bold, white letters the words, "Pay Today". There was no need to state what or to whom!

Mr Espiritu, the neighbour of Pastor Ilaw, had a responsible position in the Bureau of Public Highways. He earned a good salary but gambled and drank heavily, and was frequently late in paying his electricity bills.

Inevitably the same old rattletrap truck of the Marquez Enterprises would arrive at the middle of the month outside the home of Mr Espiritu. Pulling up beside the electricity post the driver would climb into the back of his truck and produce a ladder. Standing the ladder against the concrete post he would climb up into the tangle of wires at the top and start disconnecting the line to the Espiritu home.

By this time Mrs Espiritu, by some strange telepathy or anticipation, would appear at the window of their house and with surprising fluency would inundate the unfortunate employee of the Marquez Enterprises with a high-pitched angry torrent of words, making it very clear exactly what she thought about him, the company, Attorney Marquez and their ancestors. For the electrician it was just another professional hazard and he completed his work as quickly as possible. After a few days without electricity the bill would be paid and the same man would return in the same wheezing truck to reconnect the line.

As he watched the townsfolk coming and going beneath him in the *plaza*, setting up their stalls, decorating the official platform or heading for the homes of relatives in their most flowery clothes, Attorney Marquez caught sight of a sturdy figure striding, slowly of course in such a climate, across the *plaza* with two strong young men beside him.

"Ah, Captain Mahjong and his sons," he thought. "Better off than he was, but he'll never be more than a *barrio* headman. Strange how he brought his black sheep back under control."

Dading seemed to feel he was being looked at. He turned his head and raised a hand when he saw old Teodoro Marquez at the window.

"We'll call on Attorney Marquez later today," he said to

Berting. "It's a sad day for him. He might be grateful for some sympathy. I'll take him a copy of *Words of Comfort*, the Scripture Gift Mission booklet."

It was seeing Pedring and Berting that plunged the old man into gloom again. Perhaps the beautiful young women in their Maria Clara dresses took him back to his own Clara.

"She was a good wife," he murmured. "Why did she have to die so young? In childbirth too. So needlessly. How devastating it was to be left with the three boys, still so small. Their aunt was never able to be a proper mother to them. And no-one could take Clara's place. Miserable fate, to be singled out at thirty for such loneliness!" The bitterness he had nursed for more than forty years burned sourly in his heart again.

After Clara's death he lived only for his sons and money. Perhaps the boys would attain the ambitions he had set for himself and failed to reach. Accordingly, his eldest son, Teodoro Junior, followed in his father's footsteps as a student of law and with his father's generous support slowly climbed the slippery slope of political advancement.

"What a gift for oratory!" his father exclaimed, surprised to hear his own voice breaking through his thoughts. "And what a knack for winning popular opinion in favour of his policies for the province," he went on in silence. "His election as Governor was as good as in the bag. His campaign strategy was brilliant. There would have been a landslide victory. My hopes were within reach of fulfilment. A few more years and he could have reached the Senate. I might even have become father of the President. The opposition knew it, of course. They didn't stand a chance. They were desperate. . . ."

The old man's self pity tailed away into memories of that campaign. Great placards bearing the picture of Teodoro Junior appeared in every town and village of the province. Attractive election literature was circulated in huge quantities. Massive rallies were held when loud speakers boomed long into the night, the vigorous speeches of

Teodoro and his supporters fascinating and delighting the audiences of an extremely politically conscious people. True, there had been anger and some violence over the bank note sandwiches and free beer, but on a fine point of the law he had justified that in an enquiry and got away with it. How the support of some key men in the province had been secured would never be known. They saw to that themselves. But then fate struck again.

Teodoro Junior was on his way to address an important rally when, passing over the cursed river bridge near Santo Domingo, he ran into an ambush. His bodyguard in a following jeep had returned the fire, but too late. Teodoro Junior and two other men were killed. The driver and the rest of the passengers with him were seriously wounded.

Shrinking more and more into himself as his memories mercilessly flayed him, the old man reached for a chair and dropped into it as he recalled how yet another light in his life had been extinguished. The shock was unendurable. His second son had already died in a car accident when still a schoolboy. Little mattered to him now but his business. He was determined that none should stand in his way. He must recover his considerable financial losses sustained during the political campaign. Marquez Enterprises must be the biggest single business in the province.

From then on, Bernabe, the youngest son, had been spoiled. Unlike his eldest brother, he grew up without ambitions. If his father wanted to do nothing but make money, Bernabe liked nothing better than to spend it. Father and son were poles apart in nature and interests. While Attorney Marquez was withdrawn and left the seclusion of his home only for business appointments, Bernabe was the life and soul of every party. He studied engineering in the USA and came back with an ornate diploma and an *Americano* wife who refused to live anywhere but Manila. The "backwoods" were too primitive for her. How that had hurt the old man! Bernabe had been respectfully addressed as Engineer

Marquez just as his father and elder brother were known by the title "Attorney". With his know-how and a grant from the government under its Rural Electrification Programme, he had been able to extend the area served by the Marquez Enterprises to include a few of the larger *barrios* round Sampaguita. But dividing his time between his wife and his father was no way for a fellow to get on, even if he wanted to. The trouble was, he didn't.

"And now Bernabe is dead too, and I am left utterly alone," Attorney Marquez groaned, incapable of tears. To his few close friends it seemed that he would never recover from this latest sudden bereavement. The gaieties of the *fiesta* were the last straw.

Going over to his desk he opened the top drawer and took out a large brown envelope. It contained his passport and detailed information sent him by a travel agency. The package had arrived a couple of days ago, complete with all the visas necessary for a leisurely, luxurious, world tour.

To undertake the tour had been a difficult decision to make. Money was no object but travel abroad was still outside his experience. For weeks he had vacillated, unable to make up his mind. It was unlike him to be like this and his own indecision distressed him. Since committing himself to the venture, however, the sense of relief made him look forward to it with increasingly keen anticipation.

His doctor had been the first to suggest it. "Why not a world cruise, Attorney Marquez?" he had advised. "The change and relaxation are just what you need."

His closest friends, Judge Sarmiento and Father Areta, had agreed with the doctor, "Enjoy it while you can," they said. "There's no time like the present. Your business couldn't be going better. Leave your managers to it and pamper yourself for a change. You deserve it."

He turned the documents over, examining them one by one. "Everything tied up," he thought. "Only five more days and I'll be sailing out of Manila Bay towards Hong Kong . . . and after that Honolulu. . . ." In his imagination he was already there, seeing the exotic sights so temptingly portrayed in the brochures.

The band, still blasting away with undiminished vigour, turned the corner and shattered all possibility of day-dreams. Yawning, he replaced the package in his desk drawer. The throbbing cacophony of funfair, traffic, band and voices echoed round the lofty old house.

Pedring was puzzled. Here were fifty or sixty so-called "Bible Christians" thoroughly enjoying the *fiesta* without compromising an inch on their "impossible" principles. At the Holy Friday meeting he had decided they were deluding themselves. They could never go through with it, without offending relatives and townspeople at every turn. But here they were, more than half way through the day and not even at odds with anybody, unlike those two in the picture of Vanity Fair which Chaling and Edna had shown him. In fact they seemed to be carrying it off well.

"Hi, Captain Mahjong, make up a table with us," he had heard some of his father's old cronies call out, and Dading had answered with a cheery wave, "Thanks, but I've forgotten how to play"—excellent repartee from Santo Domingo's *mahjong* wizard.

"Hi, Celso, where're you off to?" from a crowd of red-faced rowdies clustered like flies round poor Juanita's *tuba* stall. "I've lost my thirst," came his reply, "since Jesus gave me His living water on Holy Friday!"

"Haw, haw, haw! Living water! Another glass all round, Juanita."

The bookstall flourished. Two church members served behind the counter and several aped the salesmen on the knick-knack stalls shouting out their wares. "Books, magazines! Good clean stuff you won't mind taking home to your family! Bible stories, Holy Bibles! Read it for yourself!"

An hour of that was all they could manage. They worked in relays. Most of the time one or another was busy in conversation. People seemed glad to see them there. Berting had to go home for more stock far sooner than expected.

So Pedring, aware of belonging neither to one camp nor the other, toured the fairground, watched the conjurers, avoided the friends he used to go serenading with, and drifted back from time to time to see what Edna was doing.

"I'm not a 'Bible Christian'," Edna told curious acquaintances, "but they're a decent bunch of people. You can be among their menfolk all day and never hear an off-key remark."

Pedring agreed. He was fanning himself gently with his straw hat in the shade of the jeep when Dading came and sat on a box beside him.

"Best *fiesta* ever!" Dading said, mopping his neck with a grunt of satisfaction.

"I can see it is," Pedring replied. "—for your lot."

Dading barely gave him a glance. "Yes, the *fiesta* is showing them up. 'A city set on a hill cannot be hidden.' Jesus hit the nail on the head. To me it's the same as ever, a case of *bagong nilalang*, new creation, putting new pep into everything. Can you see it happening in all these church members?"

"What worries me," muttered Pedring, "is that I can see it happening to Edna. She's hooked." But he did not seem to be complaining. Dading thought he sounded wistful.

Then Jim and Betty came by.

"We've passed out more tracts than ever before," Betty said. "And by the way, Dading, we called on Attorney Marquez. Found him quite cheerful, for him. I thought he might accept *Words of Comfort* as a gesture of sympathy. He seemed grateful."

"Just what Berting and I thought. Did Berting mention it to you?" Dading replied.

"No," Jim joined in, "Just a case of 'those who are led by the Spirit of God, they are the sons of God' I suppose."

At bedtime, late that night, Betty said to Jim, "You know, when you said that to Dading I saw such a hungry look come over Pedring's face."

The few days following the *fiesta* were all too short for Attorney Marquez, filled with busy preparations for delegating his affairs to his subordinates for four or five months at least.

The day before he was due to go up to Manila, he met again with the architect and building contractor who were to rebuild and enlarge Marquez Enterprises' main rice and animal foodstuffs warehouses. The work should be well in hand by the time he returned from abroad.

"While I am away I am to receive regular reports on the progress made," he said emphatically. "I look forward to inspecting the result and seeing the expansion project through to its conclusion when I return."

Late that night he made his way to his bedroom happy and contented. He set his alarm clock for five o'clock. "I mustn't be late getting to Manila for embarkation," he chuckled. "I'll be up in good time."

The news reached the market place soon after sunrise. From there it spread rapidly to all the *barrios*. Dading heard it from the first jeepney driver to come through to Santo Domingo for an early load of fish and travellers. Soon people were meeting each other and asking in awed tones, "Have you heard about old Teodoro Marquez?"

"Who?" Pedring asked.

"Attorney Marquez! Died in his sleep last night."

"Died!"

"Yes. When his housekeeper went to call him she found him dead in bed."

Pedring hitched the *carabao* to the sled and set off to the fields, not waiting for Berting.

"What's come over him?" Berting said to his father.

"He's gone to collect mangoes," Dading answered. "The mango tree seems to have been on his mind recently. I expect the death of Teodoro Marquez has reminded him of how we decided to cut it down if it failed to prove its worth. Since Edna prayed with Chaling he's had a lot to face up to.

"I believe he'll have something good to tell us by tonight."